Pastors Move Over

MAKE ROOM FOR THE REST OF US

A comparison of today's Church Government verses the first century Model

Written by Glen Newman

Preface

No, I do not have anything against pastors. I do believe pastors are a necessary gift given by Jesus to the Church, along with the other gifts given in Eph 4:11. I just believe they are in the wrong position within the Church's government and I have a desire to see the Five Fold ministry operated the way the believers did it in the first century church.

This book is my own personal perspective of Church structure and how church "services" were done in the Bible, and I am well aware of the lack of historical evidence available, except for what has been given to us through the Roman Catholic Church which is at best suspect. If anyone has a different viewpoint I am certainly open to discussion.

I realize with the writing of this book, I do not expect to be invited to too many Churches for speaking engagements, based on the title and subject matter alone which some pastors would find threatening to their livelihood.

The title of this book is not meant to offend anyone. Yet at times strong language needs to be spoken to get people's attention in order to make the necessary changes.

In my research the last 10 or so years I have noticed that when we measure the modern church against the first century Church in the Bible, incredibly we find many discrepancies.

The purpose for the title of this book is to grab the reader's attention before they open the pages to read, as well as to provoke thought and hopefully remove some of the blind faith we have in men's traditions.

You'll have to admit that I am not calling (as Jesus would sometimes do) anyone hypocrite, viper, or whited sepulchers. I am however trying to expose some ignorance that our modern church has toward real Biblical church government. Based on the lack of Biblical scholarship and the comfort we find in our own modern men's traditions many refuse to change.

The reason why I wrote this book is to get people to think about their own individual situation and their desire to see more effectiveness within the Church.

Jesus himself did not set out to offend the Pharisees; that was not His mission. The offense came because of their refusal to change and their stubbornness to stay with man's traditions, rather than hear the truth.

I write this book because of my love for the body of Christ and because over the years, I've seen the frustrations of many brothers and sisters sitting in the pews. People who are able and ready to minister to the body, but held back because of our traditional church governmental system; (the pastoral led church) telling them, you are not qualified as a minister, only the professionals are.

I feel I am a simple voice expressing many other believers' frustrations and making them public, where otherwise most people would keep silent.

I also feel that silence is a deadly thing for the Church. Over the centuries we have become nice quiet people who conform and don't like to stir things up or "usurp authority", which I think describes the typical sheep mentality. Yet those frustrations still remain.

The truth must be told. But if I am wrong, I will accept correction. But only if that correction comes from the Word of God, and comes in love, as I am doing my best to express myself through love at what I have found in the Word of God.

Also, this is not a sour grapes book. It is not based on bitterness or malice. But I do feel there is a need to expand the horizons of the Christian Church and ask some legitimate questions, like "How did the first century Church actually conduct their meetings and what is the difference between them and us.

Other questions would be, "Are pastors really the head of the local church?" and "Where do I fit in concerning my own ministry?"

I believe it is a healthy thing to ask these questions so that we don't get stuck in a rut and follow blindly, because the last generation did things the same way.

In fact I also hold the belief that when it comes to spiritual matters, you should never just take someone's word for it no matter how much you admire that person. Search things out in the Word for yourself. Even this book is open to and welcomes any and all scrutiny and criticism.

I don't consider myself a writer. But I'm hoping the reader will find this book easy to understand and that it stirs your heart into exploring the scriptures on these subjects more closely.

I am writing this book to the pastor who has an open mind and can look at these concepts objectively, without putting their position and salary before the Word of God.

I am writing to all those out there who have given up on the Church completely and have cut themselves off from the fellowship of other believers. There is a better way to do church and "be" the Church.

Please, don't abandon the Church all together. Start your own; in a home, a restaurant, a warehouse. Anywhere people can meet and worship the Lord and minister to one another. If you are a believer you are qualified.

Also, I am writing to all those people with gifts and callings, which are sitting in the pews wasting away, and not being recognized in your own ministry.

Lastly, I am writing these thoughts to those who have not yet been tainted by men's traditions like many young people, and those who have yet to become believers.

Long after I'm gone from this body, I pray that new generations will explore these words and unearth the Biblical way to do Church. Ministry is for all believers, not just for the few professionals.

Also, I will be using the word "he" for simplicity. I am not leaving out our sisters in the Lord. On the contrary, women are just as called and gifted as men and can be used in any and all ministries.

No doubt that the Word recognizes deaconesses, and the prophetess and all other gifts.

One last item I want to mention. I have talked with a lot of people on this subject and have found a lot of agreement, until they start examining their own church.

They would say, "Our church has small groups" or our church has a great preacher, our church is the exception."

I know that Christians are very protective and defensive of what they have settled on and chosen to believe concerning their own church system. What I am hoping for is to stir up some objectivity and discussion within the Church body. Not looking at things through the eyes of a "Baptist", "Presbyterian" or even "Charismatic".

In fact I have seen a misuse of the apostolic calling within most so called "apostolic" churches; More about that later.

I realize it is one of the hardest things for a person to do, and that is to look outside their own traditions and read the Word as it is written, but it should be done. In fact, it must be done, for the spiritual health of the Church.

I do realize that there are many interpretations out there. But that doesn't mean we stop exploring for the truth. I myself do not pretend that I have all of "the truth". But this is truly an honest revelation that God has given me.

May your search be one of excitement and discovery, and I pray that you find your own place in the Church that Jesus Himself is building.

God Bless all who read these pages.

Contact Information: Glen Newman
Phone: 1-817-573-5763
Email: glenmnewman@aol.com
Website: www.pastorsmoveover.com
Address: P.O. box 6772 Acton, TX 76049

Table of Contents

Dedication

I want to thank God for saving me through His Son Jesus Christ. I give Him all the glory for anything I do in His service. He has given me the strength and the vision to write this book for the building up of the body of Christ, so that more can realize their own gifts and callings, and therefore be fulfilled in their own individual ministries.

Secondly, I want to express my gratitude to my late wife, Juanita Presley Newman, Author of the "Reformation of the Glorious Church" which was published in 2010 just 2 months before she passed away and for 32 years of marriage, three children and eight grandchildren.

Juanita was a brilliant, anointed teacher of the Word of God. But her life was cut short by cancer. She was not quite 62 years old when she went home to be with Jesus.

I also want to acknowledge her undying dedication to the Word of God and to the body of Christ. This book is only a continuation of the great revelation that God gave Juanita concerning the fivefold ministry, which is mentioned in Ephesians 4:11.

Juanita Presley Newman

Chapter 1

Apostles

Apostles

Ephesians 4:11 and he gave some, apostles; and some
prophets; and some evangelists; and some pastors and teaches;

12 for the perfecting (To complete thoroughly, to completely
furnish) of the Saints, "FOR" the work of the ministry (This tells
me the Saints are to be doing the work of the ministry), for the
edifying of the body of Christ:

13 till we all come in the unity of the faith, and of the knowledge
of the Son of God, unto a perfect (complete) man, unto the
measure of the stature of the fullness of Christ:

14 that we henceforth be no more children, tossed to and fro,
carried about with every wind of doctrine, by the sleight of men,
and cunning craftiness, whereby they lie in wait to deceive;

15 but speaking the truth in love, may grow up into Him and all
things, which is the head, even Christ;

16 for whom the whole body fitly joined together and compacted
by that which every joint supplies, according to the effectual
working in the measure of every part, makes increase of the body
unto the edifying of itself in love.

This whole passage tells us that the apostles, prophets, evangelists, pastors and teachers are given by Jesus to build us all up, so that we, the saints are mature in the Word and equipped to do our own individual ministry.

I will be writing about each of the 5 fold ministry gifts and to hopefully show a distinction and function of each gift.

Starting with the apostle, we see a very unique individual that God uses to pioneer new territories, and plant churches where the name of Jesus has never been heard. As well as operating as a visionary for established churches in today's modern global Church.

The apostle is not necessarily a pastor, although the apostle has the ability to act as an interim pastor while getting things started in a new ministry field. In addition, it is possible for a person to have multiple gifts such as apostle/pastor or prophet/teacher. These are what I call "gift mixes".

The apostle is no more special than any other minister in the Word. They are simply pioneers who break new ground in whatever capacity that God gives them a vision for. They are the explorers of the Church.

The apostle is much like the pioneer of old who found a new land. But it takes many others to build a community, a town, and a city.

It doesn't mean that the apostle is better than the rest of the townspeople. It just means they were there first.

I would like to point out that the word apostle should normally be spelled using a small "a". I realize there are some that have a problem with ministers who call themselves an apostle. It is however, interesting that, the "titles" pastor, teacher and evangelist are widely use and accepted, with virtually no one questioning their position or their ministry.

As I read through the Scriptures I find no hierarchy in the first century Church. Although there was a leadership of elders that made up the Presbytery in the Church, these men were not CEO's, or managers of a Corporation. Instead they were fathers in the faith. They were servants to the body of Christ and love slaves for Jesus.

Jesus said those who would be great among you, must be the servant of all. Sadly, even in many circles who do believe in the apostle they have often misused the title and the office. Some have set themselves up as fancy, well dressed icons who have a "know it all attitude" and have become showmen, using the name of Jesus for their own promotion.

Some who have taken hold of the apostolic movement as traditional pastors have all of a sudden changed their title to "apostle" because it sounds grander than the title "pastor". Yet they keep the same traditional "one man" system in place. Not giving up position or authority, but giving themselves a "promotion" of such.

Here is the definition of an apostle according to Strong's concordance 652 in the Greek apostolos from 649 he is a delegate; an ambassador of the Gospel; to set apart, to send out, officially, a commissioner of Christ, a messenger.

I see nothing special about any one person having the title apostle. An apostle is simply someone who is sent out as an ambassador for Christ; someone who speaks not on his own behalf, but for Jesus Christ and for Father God. It is the same thing when our country sends a delegate or an ambassador to another country, not to represent themselves but to represent the United States.

My belief is that the problem with recognizing apostles as a viable ministry for today originated very early in Church history ,but took hold with the Roman Catholic Church and with Emperor Constantine when he legalized Christianity in his region of the world, although there were some who usurped Jesus leadership even earlier.

Constantine may have made it easier on Christians and took much of the persecution they experienced away. But being a pagan himself, (who supposedly converted to Christianity), he did not leave all his pagan practices behind. Instead he infiltrated the Church with rituals and ceremonies that polluted the Church.

One of these practices, which started even before Constantine was the elevation of a one man rule in the local church body, as well as the doctrine that there are no modern day apostles, and that they discontinued with the death of the last of the 12 apostles.

Not long after Constantine, the Roman Catholic Church started to take shape. They instituted some of the most unscriptural beliefs and practices throughout the centuries, subsequently rendering the true Church virtually nonexistent, and unrecognizable to the first century Christians.

The one-man rule was never God's intention for the Church. Jesus had discipled 12 men to say and do the things that He did, and to show the world that God works through ordinary men and women, if they are surrendered to Him and have His Spirit.

One of the most detrimental things that came from those times is that artists would put halos around the heads of Jesus, Mary and the apostles.

Now I can naturally understand honoring those in the Bible, and showing their due respect. So what's the big deal about halos in art work?

The problem is that it takes away their humanness. We must remember that the apostles were men just like ourselves, very human and with their own flaws.

I view putting a halos on people makes them almost godlike, and separates them from the rest of us mortal humans.

Remember that Mary was blessed above all women, but she was also human, born with sinful flesh like the rest of us. I also realize that Jesus was the Son of God. But He too came as the human expression of The Father in heaven. We all seem to forget the human part of Jesus. It was a man that they crucified not God.

Ephesians 4:11 He gave apostles, prophets, evangelists, pastors and teachers for the perfecting or maturing of the Saints, for the work of the ministry.

This tells me that the Saints are to be doing the work of the ministry and not just one man who has been trained to preach. Mere human beings: men and women filled with God's Spirit

Remember that God even spoke though a donkey, and he didn't have any seminary training.

Another modern concept concerning apostles in many churches is that the apostle is now the modern-day missionary. Typically, the missionary would be sent out to a foreign country far away from his own. This is all well and good, but the apostle or missionary can be sent anywhere, whether it's around the world, or across the street. To be sent does not have a measurement of distance attached to it. One is simply sent. And concerning the fact that people recognize missionaries as modern day apostles, why then call them missionaries, why not call them apostles, which is Biblical and in fact what they really are.

Visionary

In my wife's book, the Reformation of the Glorious Church, she describes apostles as those who set government in order, impart vision and train leaders. They set the direction for team ministry, and commission others for ministry and see and open new fields of ministry.

In her book she uses the following analogy that God gave her, describing the five office gifts.

A church without an apostle is like a tree without branches.

A church without prophets is like a tree un-pruned.

A church without evangelists is like a tree without fruit.

A church without pastors is like a tree without care and sustenance.

A church without teachers is like a tree without roots.

I also have my own analogy concerning the Church.

Simply put the Church has virtually three jobs besides the worship and praise of our Lord.

1. First the Church is to win souls
2. Secondly the Church is to make disciples
3. Thirdly the Church is to send out workers

Without apostolic teams of the full fivefold ministry, the potential of the Church is stagnated, stunted, and very limited, if not in numbers at least in individual spiritual growth.

The apostle is primarily kingdom minded. He can see the entire picture far beyond the four walls of the church. Billy Joe Daugherty, Willie George, Oral Roberts, and others like them are not pastors in the truest sense of the word. These men are apostles that see their mission and ministry far beyond the local church, with television broadcasts around the world, universities and many other outreaches that pastors just don't see.

The apostle also has a different influence that pastors don't have. He has open doors to kings and presidents; TV networks such as CBN, TBN and others.

Another gift that the apostle has, is finding the gifts and callings in other believers. The apostle facilitates the ministries of others within the body. The apostle doesn't hog the entire ministry spotlight for himself.

The problem though, is that the modern day apostle has been trained in the same one man pastoral system as everyone else has. It has been engrained in them throughout history to be trained as a pastor or evangelist, because that's what you do when you go to Bible college or seminary . They too have lost most of their natural gift of the biblical apostle in the process.

The Church is a family, and the apostle is like a father who raises his children to learn more and go far beyond what he was able to accomplish. His desire is that his children are more successful than he was.

And the way he accomplishes that, is to recognize their individual gifts and nurture those gifts for better productivity.

It is much like the father who is an entrepreneur who starts a father and son business, and then either turns the business over to the son as soon as he's able to run it, or he has the son start his own branch office when he is able.

Either way he doesn't wait 60 years to retire, or dies to entrust the son with any part of the family business.

Mentoring is the name of the game with the apostle. Raising up and sending out is the method of the apostle. After all, it is God's kingdom and not our own that we are trying to build up, isn't it?

If I as an apostle, raise someone up in their respective ministry and they go out to another location and start their own ministry that would bring me joy because I know I am helping increase the kingdom of God and giving Him glory.

I am not at all worried about competition, because the Church first of all should be elder led and not by one person eliminating competition in the kingdom. There is only the increasing and expansion of God's kingdom.

I have a statement that I tell people all the time concerning pastors. I tell them I can guarantee that your pastor will leave you every time without fail. He will either, die, retire, step down for whatever reason, or go to another location. He will not be at that church forever.

So where will his replacement come from in this traditional church system? In many churches they send out a call for other ministers to interview (audition) for the pastor's position. This means these candidates are in many cases strangers coming to that congregation not knowing anybody, or anything about that particular church. This also means many months or even years of getting acquainted with someone new.

With a true apostolic ministry there is mentoring and raising up of new ministers from within the local body on a continuous basis, to where a number of people can step into the place of leadership without any delay whatsoever. In truth no one will be there forever, and no one is indispensible.

Consequently, the bottom line is that no one person is the boss and therefore there is no job security issue, or jealousy, or hierarchy.

There is something else I find very interesting in the Word of God.

When Jesus taught the disciples He would teach them to do and say what He did for about a year, such as perform miracles and so on. Then He would send the disciples out; or actually "apostle" them out on temporary assignments to practice what they had learned. Jesus released the disciples after a relatively short period of time to do ministry on their own, and trusted them with that ministry. He did this even though He knew they were not ready for full time ministry, but this was still part of their training.

Obviously the disciples didn't do everything perfect, but they were learning as they went. They made mistakes and that was part of the training process.

Pastors have the hardest time releasing people into ministry. They have a tendency to micro manage everything within the local body. An apostle will teach the disciple to step out of his comfort zone and into ministry no matter what kind of mistakes they made (with corrections made along the way), so that they could learn and develop.

So by the time Jesus was lifted up into heaven to go to the Father, the only other thing needed by the disciples (students, or disciplined ones) to become apostles (Sent ones) was the baptism of the Holy Spirit. Once they were filled with the Spirit and endued with power from on high, they were ready for anything.

You can see an obvious change in Peter, from the night the Pharisees took Jesus, to the day of Pentecost. There was a definite and dramatic shift within his spirit.

This is not to say that Peter stopped making mistakes. After all he still was only human. But he was filled with power and boldness. He was filled with the Holy Spirit along with the other apostles and they were able to do great and mighty works.

I will tell you that apostles have their own flaws as well which is true of all the other ministry gifts. Apostles are kingdom minded people, and they can tend to use people to accomplish kingdom purposes. What the apostle must do is provide the people with pastors for nurture and care, especially new believers.

There are other scriptures that support the need for and recognition of apostles, prophets and other ministries within the local church.

1 Cor 12:1 Now concerning spiritual gifts, brethren, I would not have you ignorant.

Verse 4 Now there are diversities of gifts, by the same spirit.

Verse 5 There are differences of administrations, but the same Lord.

Verse 6 and there are diversities of operations, but it is the same God which works all in all.

Verse 7 But the manifestation of the Spirit is given to every man to profit withal.

Verse 8 For to one is given by the Spirit the word of wisdom; to another the word of knowledge by the same Spirit

Verse 9 to another faith by the same Spirit, to another gifts of healing by the same Spirit

Verse 10 to another the working of miracles; to another prophecy; to another discerning of spirits; to another different kinds of tongues; to another interpretation of tongues

Verse 11 but all these work that one and self same Spirit; dividing to every man severally as He will

Verse 12 for as the body is one, and has many members, and all the members of that one body, being many, are one body: so also is Christ.

Verse 13 for by one Spirit are we all baptized into one body, whether we being Jews or Gentiles, whether we be bond or free; and have been all made to drink into one Spirit

Verse 14 for the body is not one member, but many.

Verse 15 if the foot shall say, because I am not the hand, I am not of the body; is it therefore not of the body?

Verse 16 and if the ear shall say, because I am not the eye, I am not of the body; is it therefore not the body?

Verse 17 if the whole body were an eye, where were the hearing? If the whole were hearing, where was the smelling?

Verse 18 but now has God set the members every one of them in the body, as it has pleased him

Verse 19 and if they were all one member, where were the body?

Verse 20 but now are they many members, but yet one body.

Verse 21 and the eye cannot say unto the hand, I have no need of you: nor again the head to the feet, I have no need of you.

Verse 22 no, much more of those members of the body which seem to be more feeble, are necessary.

Verse 23 and those members of the body, which we think to be less honorable, upon these we bestow more abundant honor; and our uncomely parts have more abundant comeliness.

Verse 24 for our comely parts has no need: but God has tempered the body together, having given more abundant honor to that part which lacks:

Verse 25 that there should be no schism in the body; but that the members should have the same care of one for another.

Verse 26 and whether one member suffer, all the members suffer with it; or one member be honored, all the members rejoice with it.

Verse 27 now you are the body of Christ, and members in particular.

Verse 28 and God has set some in the Church, first apostles, secondarily prophets, thirdly teachers, after that, miracles, then gifts of healings, helps, governments, diversities of tongues.

Verse 29 are all apostles? Are all prophets? Are all teachers? Are all workers of miracles?

Verse 30 have all the gifts of healing? Do all speak with tongues? Do all interpret?

Verse 31 but covet earnestly the best gifts; and yet I show to you a more excellent way.

It's odd but in this chapter I don't see pastors mentioned one time. I see apostles, prophets, teachers, miracles, gifts of healing, helps, governments, tongues, but no pastors.

Also with regard to all parts of the body that were mentioned as a metaphor for the body of Christ, I do not see pastors mentioned there either.

In fact, when it comes to the modern church, where are the many members? Everything in this scripture seems to be disregarded and pastors put in as substitute for all.

This means that we have relegated and compacted virtually all of the body-ministry into one person (The pastor), and that person is only mentioned in the New Testament one time.

Let's go back to verse 14 For the body is not one member, but many. Again, where is the "many" in the modern church?

Pastors themselves will tell you that when you find a scripture in the Word of God that is mentioned over and over, or a word that is mentioned multiple times, it takes precedence over those scriptures and words that are mentioned only one time in the Word.

The word apostle, apostles or apostleship appear in the New Testament approximately 83 times. The word pastor appears only one time, which does not constitute a doctrine.

I realize that the word shepherd comes from the same word as pastor in some cases. But it is hardly used in the same context in the rest of the New Testament.

So, what is our conclusion then? Are we doing church upside down? Has satan convinced us of another way? Is there a SCHISM in the body of Christ?

In today's modern church the apostle has either been moved to the back burner of importance, or people have been convinced that they don't exist at all for today.

We all need to look into the Word of God for ourselves and explore that these ideas are incorrect.

I do not claim to be a theologian, or an expert on the Bible.
I simply read the Word and see what it says, and I am convinced
that the pastoral type of government in the Church is absolutely
unscriptural.

In addition, the pastoral government has rendered the
Church completely ineffective in the world today because the
multitudes in the pews are doing nothing to affect heaven or hell.

It has also made the Church impotent and the body of
believers, perpetual children who need constant care; spiritual
infants, if you will.

This quote from A. W. Tozer, "The modern church is in a
silo for retarded spiritual children." These are strong words from a
respected theologian of the early 20th century.

If the PASTORS would please get out of the way and
MOVE OVER FOR THE REST OF US then the Church would
recover its power and influence in the world.

The Purpose and Work
of the 5 Fold Ministry

As found in The Reformation of the Glorious Church by Juanita Newman

Apostles: Train and then commission for ministry

Prophets: Discern and confirm gifts in others. Intercede to see the plans and purposes of God.

Evangelists: Win souls and turn them over to the pastors and teachers for discipleship .

Pastors: Disciple and nurture the new believers.

Teachers: Bring believers to maturity for the work of the ministry.

Apostles: Close the circle by commissioning a new crop of believers into their place of ministry.

These office gifts working together create a Presbytery, which is the governing body of the Church, but only in an unofficial way. They are still not the bosses or hierarchy. They are simply respected members of the body who have the wisdom and experience as well as the calling to have leadership positions.

The Apostles and Prophets

Ironically still, there are scriptures that support the apostles and prophets as the foundation builders of the Church and yet we put so much credence on pastoral leadership.

Eph 2:20 ...and are built upon the foundation of the apostles and prophets. Jesus Christ Himself being the chief cornerstone.

Eph 3:5 which in other ages was not made known unto the sons of men, as it is now revealed to His holy apostles and prophets by the Spirit.

Look at the historical origins of many of our practices in the modern church chronicled in "Pagan Christianity", written by George Barna and Frank Viola, such as how pastors became the primary and central part of the ministry, while taking away the ministry from the rest of the body of Christ.

It is astounding in today's Church, with all the resources available to us that we allow these practices and this system to continue.

Let us therefore research the scriptures and see for ourselves if these things be so. Is this a revelation from God or is it from man?

Chapter 2

Prophets

Prophets

I will admit that I know less about prophets than the other fivefold gifts but I do know that my wife Juanita was very prophetic. She was able to see warning signs that no one else could see. Often she would tell me that she didn't think we should proceed with a certain purchase or activity because she got a check in her spirit. I would call those checks a red light.

I sometimes would get frustrated because I'm a go, go, go person and I don't like stop lights. We sought the Lord about the red light concept, and He showed us that normally we are usually going down the freeway of life, but then from time to time we must slow down or even stop because of obstructions in the way or warning signs.

One example that I could give you is that Juanita's friend was planning on marrying this particular guy, and the moment Juanita met him she knew that her friend was making a big mistake and should not marry this man. She saw a mask over the man's face in the spirit realm, telling my wife that he was not who he said he was and she had never met him before.

Her friend went ahead with the marriage because she loved him. But their marriage was a disaster, because his life was one lie after another. Needless to say the marriage ended in divorce.

Sadly, this was not the only time this happened.

In four other instances Juanita saw something in the spirit that told her to warn her friends of the bad relationships they were either in or about to enter. She saw the situation correctly five out of five times, yet none of her friends would listen to her, which only added to their sorrow.

The prophets in the Old Testament were typically called to serve the king or other leadership of the country. In the New Testament within the church the prophet is there for the leadership, and body of believers.

The definition of a prophet comes from Strong's concordance number 4396 in the Greek. He or she that sees and prays with prophetic insight, inspired speaker, one in front to show, to make known ones thoughts. Also he is a seer, like in the Old Testament.

The prophet sees into the future or sees the warning signs, they advise, consider, discern and behold. The prophet is like a watchman on the wall. He sees and warns of pitfalls.

The Prophet discerns error and sin, motives, callings, direction and strategies. He can see a clear division between light and dark, right and wrong.

Moses stated that he desired that all could, or would prophecy, as well as Paul talking about desiring spiritual gifts such as prophecy.

Prophesying does not necessarily make you a prophet. But, in the body, anyone has the ability to prophecy.

Most Old Testament prophets were cantankerous characters
and much of the time very hard to get along with. But they are not
there to "get along" with people; they are there to speak the truth.
They were very bold and usually fearless, and without reservation
could say, "thus saith the Lord".

There seems to be a lot of modern day prophets out there.
But what I've seen from most of them is exhortation and
encouragement of which there is nothing wrong, but I don't see
that as particularly a prophet's message or insight.

Frankly, I find it disturbing when a so called prophet or
prophetess stands before a group of believers or on television and
makes a blanket statement for the whole audience because you
support them or a friend's ministry. "God is going to bless you
beyond measure and give you the desires of your heart". Their
message usually center's around money and not the character of
the people, or the character of the country's leadership.

Their message at times in the Old Testament was very grim
and full of warning. "Come back to your Lord and serve Him or
suffer the consequences." Needless to say the prophet of old would
typically not win any popularity contests today.

I have never liked or agreed with the "hell fire and
brimstone" preaching but have we gotten so far away from the true
Word of God that we won't venture into the forbidden realm of
warning people of their sin?

Can the prophet not look into the camera or across the
congregation and say, "I see sin in the camp"?

After all the Church has become more like the world with divorce, and fornication as well as a multitude of other sins that nobody wants to talk about. We have failed to be light and salt in the world.

Are the prophets of today afraid or without the ability to say "thus saith the Lord", and not have their message tied to money, or the sale of a book? Actually it should not be an issue to use the words "thus says the Lord". After all if He said it to you then you are simply relaying a message from God. That doesn't make you special just for being a messenger.

We have a desperate need for genuine prophets in the Church today. In addition, we have a desperate need for the whole Church to know their Bible well enough to discern, distinguish, and recognize the false prophet from the real one.

Does the Church today prefer ignorant bliss over the true Word of God? Or are we to the point of no return, where we challenge no "leader" and succumb to blind acceptance.

I personally accept that there are modern day prophets, but where are they? Where are the genuine Biblical seers of today?

I pray that we all start learning more about the Word, on our own if need be, and boldly speak out against charlatans and false prophets.

My view is, even though you have charisma and put on a good show, doesn't mean the Lord approves of your message, or your methods. We need substance not performance.

I have never considered myself a prophet or even prophetic,
but I can say "thus saith the Lord". If the Church does not repent
and come out from among the world there will be consequences
for our actions. The Kingdom of heaven is at hand and we must
again become light and salt in this dark world.

Chapter 3

Evangelists

Evangelists

The word evangelist from the Greek is euangelistes which
simply means a preacher of the gospel, or good news.

The church today believes that all this preaching and
teaching that we get on Sunday and daily on the television and
radio is the gospel. It is not THE GOSPEL.

The gospel is basically Jesus Christ and Him crucified.
When Paul preached the gospel he basically gave his testimony to
unbelievers and told people that Jesus was the Christ, the true
Messiah.

The gospel or good news is that simple message that Jesus
is the Savior of the world, which is directed to the unbeliever.

The believer has already heard the message and accepted it.
So, technically what we hear in church on Sunday morning is not
the "gospel", it is teaching or preaching but not the gospel. But at
the same time I'm not denying it is good to hear or learn.

All these other messages that we hear are needed for our
growth which inspires and motivates us. They also teach us more
about the Word of God and how to live and become more like
Jesus every day.

But unless you preach Jesus is the Christ the Son of the
living God who came as a sacrifice Lamb for the sins of the world
you are not really preaching the gospel.

I'm sorry for splitting hairs but it's revelations like these that keep us on our toes scripturally, and gives us motivation to learn more about the deep things of God. Frankly I don't care if people call the other the gospel. I am simply making an observation.

The word gospel comes from the same root word as evangelist meaning to preach, to announce good news, to declare or show glad tidings, the good news. I realize there are many subjects that can be considered "good news". But when the Bible refers to the gospel or good news, it is talking about Jesus as Savior.

Without that particular good news, the fact that Jesus is the Savior for all mankind, all the other teaching that we receive is simply philosophy.

The obvious gift of an evangelist is to win souls into the kingdom of God. Their methods are wide and varied, and in many cases so are their motives depending on how they were taught.

Winning souls should never be a numbers thing, or a way to put notches on your gun. Winning souls is a ministry which is motivated by love of God, and love for people to know God.

There is nothing wrong with mentioning about the so called numbers, when you are celebrating and trying to motivate others to win souls, especially those who are not gifted as evangelists. But it is not to be a pride thing.

By the way, anyone can and everyone should win souls. But the evangelist is consumed with it to the point of it being their life message and the reason they exist.

Speaking of anyone winning souls, the easiest and best way to lead someone to Jesus is that you know this person. You work with them, or they are family members and they see your life's commitment to the Lord. All the while you can usually tell when it is the right time to lead them to the Lord.

Winning souls is the evangelists' gift and calling and they should be encouraged by the whole Church and equipped as much as possible in that calling.

Also, the true evangelist is not a "come to our church" type of minister. Instead, the evangelist is more concerned about people coming into the kingdom of God, knowing Jesus as their Savior and repenting of their sin.

There is one sad part of evangelism that I see in the modern church, and that is the lack of true discipleship, once a person becomes a believer. We will touch on that a little later in this writing.

Consequently, the evangelist can work his heart out and pray and win multitudes to the Lord and then in many cases these new converts are left on their own, like babies abandoned on the street.

New believers are essentially babies in the Lord. They need pastors for nurturing. They need teachers for foundational stability, they need to be discipled.

My observation of the modern church and its governmental structure has been, all too often, the new believer is accepted into the church but then expected to "fit in", learn our doctrine, pay your tithe, and don't ask questions that stir up controversy. I am not making this up. This type of thing really has happened.

I know that sounds a bit cynical and I wish it weren't true. But when you see it over a number of decades, then it's hard not to draw certain conclusions.

The Church was not created so that men could have secure professional careers, and receive all the adulation from the congregation and the community. That sounds too much like the Pharisee or Sadducee of old, only modernized to fit the times.

There should be a great support system around the evangelist to say to them, "if you win them, we will do everything in our power to raise them up in God's kingdom, as if they were actual physical children who need food, shelter, and especially love.

Along with the apostle, the evangelist truly brings the good news to the world.

Roman 10:14 how then shall they call on Him in whom they have not believed? And how shall they believe in Him of whom they have not heard? And how shall they hear without a preacher?

Roman10:15 and how shall they preach, except they be sent? As it is written, how beautiful are the feet of them that preach the gospel of peace, and bring glad tidings of good things.

Acts 21:8 the next day we that were of Paul's company departed and came unto Caesarea: and we entered into the house of Philip the evangelist, which was one of the seven; and abode with him.

2 Timothy 4:5 But watch thou in all things, endure afflictions, do the work of an evangelist, make full proof of your ministry.

These are a few scriptures that tell us about the work and ministry of the evangelist.

Obviously, when you speak of the modern day evangelist you think of Billy Graham. He was truly a preacher of the gospel, and ushered literally millions into the kingdom of God.

But this new generation has Reinhart Bonnke who has had phenomenal success with his gift as an evangelist.

I hope to see scores more like these men who have had basically one message, that all would come to know Jesus as their Savior and Lord.

I also hope to see others who, participate in the market place ministry, with friends, loved ones, co-workers who would speak out and say, "you too can know peace and joy by knowing the Lord Jesus Christ as your Savior.

Chapter 4

Pastors

Pastors

The word pastor in the Greek is poimen, pronounced poy-mane, meaning pastor or shepherd.

Other uses of the word were feed, herdsmen, keep, broken, company, eat, and entreat.

A primitive root; to tend a flock, i.e. pasture it; to graze; generally to rule; to associate with such as a friend, companion, keep company with, feed, use as a friend, make friendship with.

For centuries we have had pastors as the leaders of churches. Even in churches that are so big in size, they constitute a small city. It's no longer a flock, but a mega-herd, where no one gets direct nurturing from "the pastor" anymore. This is a complete distortion of the Word and the office of the pastor.

Jeremiah 3:15 and I will give you pastors according to my heart, which shall feed you will knowledge and understanding.

I don't deny the need for pastors in the Church. Scripturally, and functionally pastors are necessary for the body of Christ. But I do deny the position in which pastors have been placed. I also take issue with naming apostles, or any other of the 5 fold ministry pastor, just because they have been trained in the traditional way we are all familiar with.

It seems anyone who has gone to seminary, Bible College or some other institution of higher learning where the training in the Bible is concerned, people just naturally call them pastor.

Sadly, the modern western world lacks the knowledge and finds little value in the meaning of words. As a result the biblical language suffers dramatically.

Tradition removes the "WHY" out of our lives. Because it calcifies our actions with rote memory and wipes out the history of how we got there in the first place. The solution would be simple if we could just find more motivated thinkers in the body of Christ. Recognizing the true and legitimate ministry of every believer is a start. I believe people wili then take ownership of their own ministry and the kingdom of God, resulting in greater effectiveness in the Church as a whole.

An example of the traditional method is that even cattle know where to go to get the hay or grain, because they've been there so many times before. Besides, the younger ones don't even need to know where the food is, because they're following the others who do know.

Our personal knowledge of the Word has suffered greatly, because it has been relegated to a small minority of men throughout history who have withheld that knowledge because they felt the common man could not rightly interpret the Word.

After centuries, the common man simply accepted this position of subordination and substitutional ministry, even after he had received full access to the Word during the Reformation.

The typical Christian had been conditioned into serving in a spectator roll. That was not the case in the 1st century Church.

Today, we have no excuse and have every opportunity to study the Word for ourselves. But for the masses, there has been a lack of motivation to move out of the status quo and into their own gifts and callings.

Regrettably, the majority has handed over their own ministries within the Church to the one man system of church government which is the whole point of this writing.

In all practicality, there is no way that one person can "pastor" so many people. The true pastor in reality is a small group minister who can tend the sheep, because they are able to know the sheep intimately.

Historically pastors have been the ones who receive the largest salaries, the ones who are in charge, the ones who do the counseling, and are responsible for every detail in the local church. They are also the ones who do the preaching and are looked to for most all the spiritual answers.

Essentially, in most people's eyes around the world, the pastor is the number one person to go to for all spiritual guidance. He is the one to learn from and the one person with all the authority in the local church, and he is the "man of God".

Also the pastor must have papers saying he is ordained and licensed in his profession before his hired. In many cases the main person in this position is referred to as the senior pastor, if there are multiple ministers on staff.

In all of the above description neither person can be found in the Bible. He simply did not exist.

In the New/Testament church pastors, (plural) were simply available to small groups, such as house church settings. No one knows how many people were under the pastor's care, but these groups were small in number and scattered throughout the city. Collectively these congregations were considered one church within that particular city.

The Church of Ephesus, the Church of Corinth, and all the other New Testament churches were described by Paul in the singular, even though they met in multiple locations, such as house to house. So there were multiple pastors.

The pastor's primary gift and calling is his nurture and care of the Saints. In today's church you can have hundreds and even thousands of pastors (male and female) in the so called mega church setting, sitting in the pews doing nothing, because they are not recognized or encouraged in their ministry.

I find it absurd that people expect one person to "nurture" thousands. So the question arises" how can you nurture someone if you don't even know their name?"

Nurture is a gift that is an intimate and a one on one ministry. The pastor is a father or mother figure within a close knit group that can be depended upon for any type of spiritual guidance, correction, instruction and most of all love.

The pastor is there for you 24/7, because their motivation is love. Being a pastor is not a profession, it is a calling and a gift. A person cannot be trained to be a pastor it is a gift within them. That is who they are.

I have personally seen evangelists who were called pastor and I've also seen prophets with the same title.

In the case of one evangelist that I knew who was called pastor, he was very miserable in that position. He was called to be an evangelist. His gift was evangelism, and no amount of training or salary would put the gift of pastor inside him.

Fortunately he quit his position as pastor and went back out on the road as an evangelist. He was much happier being who he was.

In the case of prophets who are called pastor; that can literally leave permanent scars on people.

A prophet is typically not a nurturing person by nature. That is not usually their gifting, unless of course they have the "GIFT MIX" of prophet and pastor, which is highly unlikely, and rare.

I'm not saying it cannot happen, or that there are not people out there who are both prophet and pastor. But it is a rare sight indeed.

Prophets typically are gifted with the uncanny ability to see danger ahead. They are also acutely aware of sin in the body. The prophet's gift is to warn and to correct.

The pastor is almost on the opposite side of the prophet, being more of an enabler than one who exposes sin.

Most people don't enjoy or even like hearing from the truly Biblical prophet, because they see the prophet as a doom and gloom type person. They are also, not typically the most amiable people in the world.

My point is that you can give the title pastor to a prophet, but he is still a prophet by nature.

The word pastor basically means the shepherd feeding his flock, Not a CEO of a mega-church, corporation, or conglomerate.

The true pastor is a father or mother in the faith, who nurtures a small number of people, such as a house church.

Pastors or shepherds know their sheep intimately. Jesus said, my sheep hear my voice and He is the Great Shepherd.

God can handle His flock, but men are not equipped to "pastor" a mega flock.

The flock should be manageable, and pastors are to be intimately close to the sheep. So close, they know them by name and they are like a family member, they know their joys, their hurts, the successes and failures of each person.

Truthfully in a church of about 1000 people, there should be no less than 10 pastors.

At the risk of repeating myself, I ask the question, "How can any one person nurture 1000 people?"

I have another question. "How many sheep does a shepherd have to have before he CAN'T keep track of them anymore?" Or, "how many sheep does he have to manage before he DOESN'T see them wondering off, spiritually speaking, or otherwise?"

It is virtually impossible for some of these ministers of large churches to feed and nurture the hundreds and sometimes thousands of sheep under their care, and yet we call these people "pastor".

When I say, feed the flock, I mean that it is much more than preaching a sermon each Sunday morning. I'm sure you would have to admit that is not nurture, it is preaching.

Those who are in charge of house churches or small groups, who spiritually feed the flock, should be recognized as pastors, not as cell group leaders or some other modern clinical name that we give them.

They are not recognized as pastors because we don't want to give them too much recognition and threaten the senior pastor's position and authority. I'm sorry if that sounds harsh, but I can't see any other reason for this lack of importance that is placed on the small home church meeting.

Going to a Bible college or seminary does not make you a pastor. Having a heart to feed and protect the flock does.

Pastors are not professionals with degrees, but fathers and mothers who would lay down their lives for the sheep.

In Pagan Christianity (by Barna and Viola), there is a great chapter concerning pastors and their historical rise to pre-eminence. It is, to say the least, very revealing.

It is amazing to me how we can read the scriptures, for so many centuries and still overlook such a primary part of our faith, the "governmental structure" of the Church.

My only answer is that the Church has been dummed down for so long concerning the knowledge of the scriptures we have simply gone along with those who are supposed to be teaching us the Word of God properly.

After all, these are the so called caring ministers that we hire for comfort, counsel, spiritual leadership, and Biblical training. Why should we question their motives, position and authority or anything they say.

But, they are also the ones who would lose their jobs, if people only knew better.

The priesthood is for all believers, and not a select few who are the elite, when it comes to spiritual matters.

Today, in the 21st century, we have every imaginable resource at our fingertips, literally. I do encourage education as much as possible, but not at the expense of the Spirit of God working within the Church, which is God's people.

We do not have any excuse not to learn Greek and Hebrew, and to delve deep into the scriptures to find things out for ourselves. We can get an entire Biblical education through a multitude of resources.

Or have we become so indoctrinated, lazy, or apathetic, that we just don't care if it's right or wrong? "Just let me keep my tradition, leave me alone and don't make waves."

I sincerely hope there are some people out there who want to get back to, not only true worship, but also true church government, where every member really is a minister, rather than it being just a nice slogan on a banner on a wall in the sanctuary.

The position and prominence of the pastor literally stands in the way of everyone being a minister and priest in the church body by the very inherent nature of that position.

The church should be elder led which inherently prevents pride on the part of the one man government the pastor and causes each elder to defer to one another as they operate like true Biblical elders and not like a "board".

If we could only look into the scriptures and extract from our modern traditions everything that is not scripturally based, we would have the most pure church history has seen in centuries.

If only someone would have the courage to stand up and speak out as they are led by the Spirit and not their own ego to bring the Church back to its New Testament roots.

It's doubtful at this present time that a pastor would find such courage. But, the Spirit of God can lay this burden on anyone's heart. Nothing is impossible with Him.

Fortunately, there are some people out there who have caught this vision. Although few in number, the vision is growing and we will see some day, a Church where all are ministers, and all have a place of recognition in the body.

I also am aware that things will be done wrong in some areas. But that is a part of our learning process. Admittedly, we've never done it the true Biblical way, so there will be a lot of controversy and disorganization while we sort things out. But I think it's worth the effort.

After all, we have been doing a lot of wrong things for 17 centuries and more. So why not start now, and maybe we'll look more like the Bride of Christ so He will actually be able to recognize His beloved when He returns.

Chapter 5

Teachers

Teachers

Besides being apostolic in my gifting, I am also a teacher. I can't help it. It's in my blood. I've always had this great desire to take those who don't know and bring them to a point where they feel comfortable with whatever it is we are learning.

Whether it is young people learning about soccer or baseball, or others who desire to learn more about the Word of God, it is a gift that God has given me, ever since I can remember.

I suppose part of it comes from being a student myself. The curiosity I have for the Word guides me and when I've discovered something, I have a desire to share that revelation with others.

A teacher in the Bible or at least in the Jewish nation was called a Rabbi. He was a coach, a guide and instructor, a mentor.

One primary attribute of a teacher is the desire for Biblical accuracy to the best of his ability. Opinions are worthless to the teacher. If it doesn't say it in God's Word then it doesn't bear repeating.

Also, a true teacher is always learning. If there is a new revelation that someone has discovered, the teacher will research it's accuracy with the Word of God and adjust their teaching accordingly, even if it means admitting that they were wrong.

True Bible teachers do not care about denominational doctrines, but only what is in the Word of God.

The teacher or rabbi, and the pastor are needed in the church for nurture, guidance, training and discipleship.

The teacher is there to help the new believer rightly divide the Word of Truth, and to become strong enough in the Word so as to be able to renew their mind, and withstand the wiles of the devil.

Jesus as the teacher or rabbi was there to duplicate himself. The disciples were to become just like Him. He expected it and He expects us to do the same.

The only thing we cannot do with regard to being "like" Jesus is that we were not born sinless, and we cannot die for anyone else's sins. Other than that He truly expects us to be just like Him.

The teacher is like a coach, training believers in the fundamentals of the Word.

When a little league coach teaches the fundamentals of baseball, he teaches so many basic things, like how to throw a ball, how to catch a ball, and how to hit. The movements on the field gradually come together until instinct takes over. That instinct is what we should possess when it comes to the Word of God.

When Jesus was tempted in the wilderness, He was so full of the Word, that He didn't panic and run to His pastor for counsel. Instead, instinctively He quoted the Word, "man shall not live by bread alone, but by every Word that proceeds out of the mouth of God".

Teachers help provide spiritual strength to all who want to know the Word better. They put roots to people's faith, and help them become grounded so they are not tossed to and fro by every wind of doctrine.

I have a desire to take a group of young, new believers and pour into them the Word, in the way Jesus did, and watch them blossom into strong, spirit filled, spirit led believers who are not weak babies after a number of years, but are ready to stand for the sake of the gospel.

It is my contention, that every local church no matter how small should have its own Bible school, institute, or training center, to teach and disciple all the believers.

There is a crisis in the Church today, all over the world. People do not know their Bible, and when things get tough, they will not know how to stand in the face of adversity. They're always desiring milk and never able to handle meat.

Besides Islam growing, there is also a big anti Christ spirit in the world today; So many people denouncing Jesus as The Christ and becoming atheists, humanists, or making up their own religion. Without the Word, how will a person withstand all the fiery darts of the enemy?

I wonder sometimes with the way things are going in our country and in our world today. Will the Church eventually have to go underground? History proves anything is possible.

I am not talking about China, or North Korea. I am talking about the United States of America and the rest of the western world. We can no longer be completely sure. That is why we need to know our Bible as much as possible.

While some are preaching prosperity, there are other scriptures that talk about wars and rumors of wars. Also still, other scriptures that mention the persecution of the Church.

I am not a doom and gloom person. But we must also not stick our head in the sand because we don't like to hear certain scriptures, namely the hard ones.

Which message is correct? If we don't have teachers to train us in the whole Word as well as the Holy Spirit being our teacher sent by God, we will not know.

Teachers are a vital part of the Body of Christ. I'm not talking about Sunday school teachers, although they have their place. I am referring to called, anointed teachers, who have a burden to "train up the child in the way he should go and when he is old, he will not depart from it.

The teacher is like any other gift given by Jesus. They are consumed with the desire to teach, and train any and all who would be hungry enough to learn the Word of God.

Teachers are also students of the Scriptures. Otherwise, how would they be able to teach and what would they teach? You can't give what you don't have.

There are a couple of ways I like to study the Bible. One being word studies. Even though I don't know Greek or Hebrew, there are resources that I use to learn the meaning of certain words.

This is an exciting way to learn more about the Word. To find out what the author meant when he used a certain word, and the context in which that word was used, is very rewarding. It's like finding gold or some historical artifact that was lost for centuries.

One example is the word "believe". It actually means to trust in, rely upon, and adhere to. The word "believe" is much more than mental assent to God. If you believe there is an unquestionable faith and trust. There is reliance in Him, His wisdom, and His word. In addition, the word "believe" carries with it an unwavering obedience to God and His Word.

There I go, teaching again. My point is that no one has to give you an assignment to teach if you are a true teacher. It just comes out.

Another way to study, is slowly reading the scriptures one verse after the other, keeping the entire subject in context. Do you realize that even though our Bibles are separated into chapters and verses, some thoughts should not have been cut off by the end of a verse or chapter?

For instance, look at the "therefore" in the Bible, especially at the beginning of a chapter. What was said before that? Therefore what?

Isn't it when you use the word therefore, that is a continuation of a thought? Why would you then start a chapter or verse in the Word of God with "therefore"? It doesn't make sense unless you look at the whole context which is what was said prior to "therefore".

I recognize this little exercise is basic for some, but others who read this may not have realized the afore mentioned fact.

I must say too, that a teacher is not a teacher until something is learned. That is probably part of the reason so many students fail in school.

The person can go through the text book, give all the tests, and have the students recite volumes. But if the one being "taught" doesn't get it, then you haven't taught a thing.

A teacher knows that every person is an individual, and that everyone learns by different means and methods. One size does not fit all.

My wife Juanita was one of the best teachers I've ever known. When we first met, I was the new youth pastor and she was in charge of children's church. To show you the extreme teacher in her, I will list a number of her ways and methods that she would use.

First she would write the lesson. She didn't get it out of a book written by Christian publishers.

Then she would hand make puppets. Next she would make the set, such as cut out plywood in the shape of a train and paint it. Then she would recruit others to learn a script which she would write as well.

This is just the beginning. She would then teach the same scriptural principle, using no less than four different methods. If the children didn't understand using the puppet show, then there was a skit, then a simple reading and repeating the scriptures, and finally a song, which she would also write, that reinforced everything.

Through the contests and sometimes just silliness, every child had an opportunity to learn that Bible principle in his own medium. They learned, therefore she taught.

I believe that is why Jesus was such an excellent teacher. He used different methods to show 12 different people who He was and why He was here. In addition, He used the method of letting His disciples do things for themselves. He let them make the mistakes that were required for some of them to learn.

A carpenters apprentice will not learn how to be a great carpenter if all he does is play fetch for the one who is actually doing the carpentry. The apprentice needs to do hands on training, cutting boards too short, making the wrong measurements and so on.

This same principle applies to every part of life, especially spiritual matters. Doing is learning. If you sit in a pew for 40 years and do nothing, you have learned less spiritually than the 20 year old who is doing, and applying and stepping out into new horizons.

In addition, although this person is younger, he will more than likely be the more mature one spiritually, than those who sit idle. Regrettably, the pastoral position prevents or at least retards spiritual maturity by its very existence. It hobbles the majority of the body of Christ and steps in and takes over their ministry.

Intense Bible training and discipleship are the keys to spiritual maturity, active involvement, and growth within the Church.

Chapter 6

Bishops and
Presbyters

Bishops and Presbyters

The word bishop comes from the Greek word episkopos, meaning overseer.

The word presbyter comes from the Greek word presbyterion meaning the order of the elders.

Overseers and Elders are the basic meaning of Bishop and Presbyter. They are virtually the same thing.

Acts 20:28 take heed therefore unto yourselves, and to all the flock, over which the Holy Ghost has made you overseers (the word which also means bishop) to feed the Church of God, which He has purchased with His own blood.

These days' bishops and presbyters are equivalent to corporate middle managers of denominations, who know little or nothing about the local congregation except what they see on paper. They are seldom within the local body but instead oversee large regions where they have limited acquaintance with each church because there are so many.

It is a travesty for these so called "ministers" to be so far removed from the local body, and yet wield so much power over it, by telling them such things as how to conduct services or administer communion, or whatever.

Bishops and presbyters in the first century were part of the
local body, ministering just like everyone else, they were the
elders. There was nothing special about these people other than age
and maturity in the Word.

However I do recognize the authority of the apostles who
were in Jerusalem and Paul who oversaw several churches from
afar. But that was in a fledgling Church that had not yet worked
out all the kinks of the new covenant. In addition Paul had a
vested interest in the churches he oversaw.

The Roman Catholic church has wrecked the Word of God
and distorted positions and titles in the Bible so that our entire
society has been convinced of so many falsehoods and lies.

Example: Where in the Word of God can we find the word pope?
Who is this person suppose to represent?

The terms or positions of bishop, presbyter, and elder are
basically synonymous terms. Remember there is no hierarchy in
the Bible. No managers, or bigwigs, just the local body that had
elders who were accountable to God for the accuracy of the Word
and the   behavior of the body.

They took their positions and responsibilities very
seriously, and guarded the truth of the Word with their lives. It
wasn't just their job, or occupation but their deep conviction that
Christ was the head of the Church and they were responsible to
Him.

Wouldn't it be refreshing to see true Biblical bishops and presbyters who have no sense of hierarchy or separation from the body because of their position or title?

I remember during the 1980"s there was this whole submission doctrine going around. The premise of the teaching was that those who were new, younger and less informed were required to submit to the older, more established Christians. This is a Biblical principle, except that it was abused and a one sided, pride filled doctrine.

You literally had people demanding things of others, as if they were their servants. Then if the person didn't fulfill the needs of the elder, then they were considered rebellious and un-submissive. After all these were generals in the body of Christ. Unfortunately the Bible doesn't say anything about generals in the Church although we are to respect the elder. Conversely the elder is to be the greater servant according to the way Jesus described it.

All the while the Word saying if you would be great in the kingdom, become the servant of all. That is why Jesus washed the disciple's feet. Not to set up some strange ceremony where people actually wash each other's feet. But to show the elder, the more mature, the one who is the teacher to humble themselves and lay down their lives for the brethren. We are all to submit to one another.

Remember that true leadership in the Church is unlike the world. It is servant-hood and submitting to each other. A great bishop or presbyter is also a great servant to the body.

The qualifications of a bishop are in 1 Timothy 3:1-7. This is a true saying. If a man desires the office of a bishop, he desires a good work.

V2 A bishop then must be blameless, the husband of one wife, vigilant, sober, of good behavior, given to hospitality, apt to teach;

V3 Not given to wine, no striker, not greedy of filthy lucre; but patient, not a brawler, not covetous;

V4 One that rules well his own house, having his children in subjection with all gravity;

V5 For if a man know not how to rule his own house, how shall he take care of the Church of God?

V6 Not a novice, lest being lifted up with pride he fall into the condemnation of the devil.

V7 Moreover he must have a good report of them which are without: lest he fall into reproach and the snare of the devil.

Also Titus 1:6-9 If any be blameless, the husband of one wife, having faithful children not accused of riot or unruly.

V7 For a bishop must be blameless, as the steward of God; not self willed, not soon angry, not given to wine, not given to filthy lucre;

V8 But a lover of hospitality, a lover of good men, sober, just, holy, temperate;

V9 Holding fast the faithful word as he hath been taught, that he may be able by sound doctrine both to exhort and to convince the gainsayers.

These qualifications are clear and precise. They leave no room for the prideful, domineering, ambitious person who cares more for status than the Kingdom of God.

Chapter 7

Elders

Elders

The word elder comes from the Greek word meizon pronounced, (may zon); Which means larger or greater, especially in age.

Another word in the Greek that is translated elders is presbyteros also meaning elder, older, a senior.

In ancient days there was a respect of elders that we don't see in America today. Even in other societies, there is respect shown to elders, which you can't find in the western culture.

My personal example is, when I was growing up, you called your elders sir and ma'am. Today I can go into a store, (and I have just turned 60) and some 16 year old kid will look up and ask, "Can I help you buddy?"

Respect of the elders is all but gone in our world today. But in the days of the Bible and in that society elders were honored and respected as fathers and mothers.

It is not that the elder makes a demand for honor, but by the simple fact that they have journeyed this earth longer and have more experience, they have earned the respect that is due them.

Along with the respect and honor comes a greater responsibility to the body of Christ to be an example of godliness and humility.

Peter's exhortation to the elders in the Church

1 Peter 5:1 The elders which are among you I exhort, who am also an elder, and a witness of the sufferings of Christ, and also a partaker of the glory that shall be revealed.

1 Peter 5:2 Feed the flock of God which is among you, taking the oversight thereof, not by constraint, but willingly: not for filthy lucre, but of a ready mind.

1 Peter 5:3 Neither as being lords over God's heritage, but being examples to the flock.

1 Peter 5:4 And when the Chief Shepherd shall appear, you will receive a crown of glory that fades not away.

1 Peter 5:5 Likewise, you younger, submit yourselves to the elder. Yes, all of you be subject one to another, and be clothed with humility: for God resists the proud, and gives grace to the humble.

1 Peter 5:6 Humble yourselves therefore under the mighty hand of God, that He may exalt you in due time:

1 Peter 5:7 Casting all your care upon Him; for He cares for you. Today, we are apt to only hear that last verse in a sermon, as a scripture of comfort without the context of the other verses above instructing the elders to behave as servants to the flock.

This is why knowing scripture is so important, but knowing full passages is a high priority. The reason being, you can know a scripture, but if you don't know the context, you can easily be led astray.

The elders are the responsible ones who hold the truth in their hands. If they are deceived then the whole Church can be led in the wrong direction.

The power of positive thinking has crept into the Church and taken it over. I do believe in positive thinking, as I equate it with faith. But that is not the whole counsel of God.

The so called "Full Gospel Churches" are nothing of the sort. They basically have 3 messages.

1 If you tithe and give, God will bless you ie the prosperity message

2 Think only positive thoughts. Anything else is a lack of faith

3 Divine healing

These are all good messages, but there is so much more to the Word of God and we must search it all out, not just the scriptures that comfort us.

My point is, this is not the full gospel. There are things in the Word of God that sometimes don't seem pleasant to hear, but we must preach the entire Word of God.

That is why I have a hard time with specialists who only have one message. We have so many specialists, that you have to listen to a multitude of teachers and preachers to get all of the Word.

In fact there is one preacher on TV in particular that preaches the same feel good message every time they fill the church.

I wonder sometimes how he can keep an audience after even 3 months of hearing that same message over and over again. It's not even packaged differently.

Are the people deaf, or are they just not very committed to the Word? How spiritually mature can they be after hearing such basic Biblical principles week after week? I pray that church has some small groups or home churches that get to the rest of the Bible.

There are a few good teachers on TV. But for the most part, you're getting a narrow, specialized message that lacks the fullness of the whole Word of God.

There is another way if the Church would make it available. You could sit under the elders in your local church and learn line upon line, precept upon precept, asking questions and challenging what you don't understand which is a great way to learn all of the Word. That is if you could find a church that is structured that way.

Remember, you the elders are responsible, along with the teachers who in most cases could be the same people.

Chapter 8

Deacons

Deacons

The word Deacon comes from the Greek word diakonos, pronounced (de aw kon os) meaning minister or servant, to run errands, an attendant, a waiter.

Deacons are different from elders. Although the only distinction that I can find between the two is, that the elder is obviously older but not necessarily more spiritually mature. In addition, the elder typically takes care of the spiritual needs of the body and the deacon the physical needs of the body.

Stephen was the most noted deacon in the Bible. He was called the first martyr of the new Christian church. He lost his life for his strong defense of the gospel.

Although Stephen was chosen among others to take care of what we would consider menial tasks, he was one of the most powerful figures to emerge from those believers.

Stephen preached one of the longest sermons in the New Testament and he was fearless in the face of death.

Deacons do take care of the physical needs of the Church. But they must be people of character, faith, and power.

The deacon is in the trenches with the day to day activities, and they don't get much recognition or seem so spiritual, but are the literal hands and feet of what we call the ministry.

It's not hard to imagine that deacons fit in well with the helps ministry, which is our next chapter.

The deacon is typically a behind the scenes minister. He could be a cook, or a sound man, or a custodian. But the main thing is, he is there when you need him.

By the way, I don't want to leave out our sisters. When I use the word "he" I mean the whole body of Christ including women. For me it's just simpler to say he. That includes all ministries within the body.

Some of the qualifications of a deacon are as follows. 1Timothy 3:8-13 Likewise must the deacons be grave, not double tongued, not given to much wine, not greedy of filthy lucre;

V9,10 Holding the mystery of the faith in a pure conscience. And let these also first be proved; then let them use the office of a deacon, being found blameless.

V11 Even so must their wives be grave, not slanderers, sober, faithful in all things.

V12 Let the deacons be the husband of one wife, ruling their children and their own houses well.

V13 For those who have used the office of a deacon well, purchase to themselves a good degree, and great boldness in the faith which is in Christ Jesus.

Being a deacon or deaconess is an admirable office and a much needed position in the Church. There is nothing else I have to add, since this is not a comprehensive study on each ministry within the Church.

Chapter 9

Helps

Helps

The word helps comes from the Greek word boetheo pronounced (boy theo) meaning to aid or relieve.

All of the fivefold ministry's need the helps ministry. Without helps all of the work in the Church grinds to a halt or is severely hindered, because it takes everyone working as a body to minister to the Church and to preach the gospel to the unbeliever.

I like using the illustration that sometimes when there is a fellowship dinner, or a potluck if you will, there are people who do the set up and the cooking and cleanup afterwards.

After everyone is finished eating and many are lingering and fellowshipping, you can hear chairs in the background being neatly put away and the place being cleaned up.

These helpers don't need anyone to tell them to do the cleanup. That is simply their ministry gift and it comes to them naturally, and from the heart.

Helpers usually do not want to preach or teach a class or be in front of a crowd of people. But you can give them a task that is necessary to be done in the Church and they are happy to do it with all their might.

There is a multitude of helps type activities, from cleaning, to scheduling events and set up, too numerous to mention. I will also add that no one is above doing any activity in the church including the apostles, pastors, or prophets. Remember, there is no hierarchy in Jesus' Church, except for The Father, Son and Holy Spirit.

But at the same time each ministry has its own place, its function, and its usefulness.

I can fully appreciate the helps ministry because without helps not much gets accomplished in the Church.

If you think of all the things that the helps ministry is involved in within the Church, you would lose count. It would be too numerous to consider.

From maintaining buildings, to making schedules, and everything in between, the helps ministry is highly valued and should be recognized as such in the Body of Christ.

That is all I will say about this ministry, because we have been trying to concentrate on the governmental structure of the Church and not give an exhaustive study on each ministry.

Chapter 10

Some how-to's

Some How-To's

We already know how to "do" church the traditional way, where everything is scheduled and predictable within any given service. The Holy Spirit usually is disregarded in these meetings, because we have our own agenda of how the service should go, especially those that have multiple services and are constrained by time to end so another group of people can be herded in to hear the same song's and sermon.

How do you do church if it's not a pastoral led service with the usual predictable activities? Typically you're ushered to your seat and there are songs, announcements, an offering. Then comes the sermon and prayer, then we're all released to go home or invited for pot luck. It's all too predictable. Where, I would ask is 1Cor 12 and 14 and where is the Holy Spirit?

I have had friends who are pastors, that have read my wife's book "The Reformation of the Glorious Church" and they reply, "This is a great book, but how do you implement it? Answer: 1 Cor 12 and 14.

We realized then, that being strictly "Pastors" in their gifting, they would have no clue how to put forward an "Apostolic" vision.

These men are pastors, and I might add very good pastors. But that is where the problem lies. Without possessing the gift of an apostle, the pastor cannot see beyond the boundaries of the sheepfold.

It would be like asking a brilliant computer scientist to write and perform a symphony. If the gift is not in you it is impractical to require you to operate with excellence, or even passion for that matter.

Obviously, if a pastor has the gift "MIX" of apostle/pastor, he would be able to see outside the four walls of the church and put the vision God gave him into practice. But you cannot set forth things that you cannot envision.

When I mention gift mixes, I am saying that everyone is different and individual in all that they are and all that they do. That includes spiritual gifts. It is possible to have multiple gifts. That is why I use the term gift mixes.

There is no hard rule about spiritual gifts, and I don't want people to think that we are putting people in a box when we describe them as pastor or prophet or whatever. But what I am saying is that certain gifts in a person can be more prominent than others.

Jesus himself operated in all of the gifts as it relates to Eph 4:11. He was an apostle of God, "sent" to earth to do His mission for the Father. He was a prophet and an evangelist as He would invite others "come follow me".

Jesus was and is our teacher as well as the Holy Spirit. Finally, He was a pastor, being our Great Shepherd.

The only way to implement things beyond the pastor's vision is to have an apostle or apostles in the body, with whom the pastor will listen. That is if you are still operating in the pastoral led church.

If the apostle is not listened to, or for that matter any other ministry such as prophets, then that church will only operate in one dimension and never reach its full potential.

Now when I say, have apostles in the body, I mean someone who either started that church or an apostle that is locally connected to that body who has a vested interest and close relationship with that body of believers.

Some churches have tried to enlist everything from traveling evangelists, or teachers, to big name ministries to be their "apostle". This never seems to work because these people virtually have nothing invested or at stake in that body. They may help as an interim apostle, but there needs to be a much closer connection in the long run.

If we would all learn to recognize and respect each other's gift, callings, and ministries and remove ourselves from the traditional pastoral led ministry, there would be greater effect, and power in the Church as a whole. Remember it is His Church not ours.

How do you do Church?

1 Corinthians 12 and 14

1 Cor 14:26 How is it then, brethren, when you come together, every one of you has a psalm, a doctrine or teaching, has a tongue, has a revelation, and has an interpretation. Let all things be done unto edifying.

It is amazing to me that this scripture has been there, in writing for 2000 years, and yet we conduct church like we are in a classroom. This scripture has virtually been ignored for the last 1700 years.

When I say we conduct church classroom style, I mean, the whole congregation is set up like an audience for listening only, not participation or interaction. In addition, the people on the platform basically become performers.

Obviously it would be virtually impossible for each member to contribute individually, like having a song, a teaching, a revelation, or an interpretation, when you have a congregation of several thousand people. Or for that matter just a couple of hundred people.

Please don't misunderstand. I am not against corporate praise or worship no matter what the size of the congregation. That is not what we are talking about here. I am talking about having church where everyone has the opportunity to minister and to be ministered to and keeping these groups (churches) small enough to accomplish just that.

What I am saying is, in the normal day-to-day coming together of the Saints for worship and praise and to minister to one another, to pray for one another, it should be in a small group gathering. The Word says, "When two or three are gathered in my (Jesus) name, there am I in the midst of you". That is church.

Some churches have what they call cell groups or cell churches or even house churches. Whatever you call the group, it is the church coming together worshipping the Lord, edifying one another, teaching and discipling one another. It's the Saints doing the ministry, not the professionals.

If the pastor insists on keeping the tradition going within the four walls of the church building, there can at least be this extension, which will enrich that body more than they could ever imagine. But the leadership has to place a high priority and great importance on these small meetings for the congregation to view them with importance.

The pastor can retain his position and salary, which is in fact unscriptural, but nonetheless exists, while the believers can grow outside the church building and be used of God.

If the Saints are coming together with these purposes in mind and not just for fellowship, then they are applying and implementing 1 Corinthians 14:26. They are having church.

Besides, many people don't realize it, but the best fellowship you can ever have, is in the Word of God with other believers.

Another thing worth mentioning is that these home gatherings or house churches should not be run by a pastor or teacher standing up and preaching or teaching to everyone present without the interaction of everyone's gifts being used. This is simply doing church the traditional way but just changing locations.

All the believers must have an opportunity to share what God has given them, and to pray for one another, teach one another, disciple one another and freely operate in the gifts of the Spirit.

The people can ask questions and even challenge one another if some of what is being said doesn't sound right to them. You have full discussion and full participation. 1 Cor 12 & 14.

In this type of gathering everyone has an equal footing to minister, no matter how immature or young in the Lord they are. New Christians should be encouraged to use their gifts and not hold back just because they're new believers. This is how they learn to do things scripturally.

With the elders present there can be oversight (bishops and presbyters) and correction done immediately if something is said or done un-scripturally.

I realize that you do not let a novice teach, but that doesn't mean they cannot contribute. And sometimes the new believer can have a greater revelation than the older ones, so encouraging them to share, helps in their spiritual growth.

Another issue that we face is "what do we call these meetings?" I prefer to use the term church, or house church or home church. I prefer using these terms over cell groups, or something else someone has made up, which waters down what it actually is. Besides it is a true Biblical term. If people are having church in their home, then call it church. Church is not a cell, although I know why this terminology was originally adopted.

It is my opinion the use of the word cell group separates it from what they consider real church by a level of importance in people's minds. We do "real church" at the big church building. Everything else is extra- curricular and not as important.

After all, tradition says, you can't "do church" without a pastor present, and you can't "have church" anywhere except in the church building.

In reality, in most people's minds there is more prestige attached to the church building then that of a house or a restaurant or some other location. When you think about it, the absurdity of this kind of thinking is mind boggling.

Did Jesus, **not** "have church" unless He was at the Synagogue? Was His Sermon on the Mount not as viable unless He was surrounded by four walls?

Why is it any different for us today? And finally, why does the pastor have to be in charge and micro- manage everything? Is his ego so fragile that unless he oversees every activity in the church, then there is no credibility attached to it?

We are "The Church" and not a building and we must take back our rightful place in the Kingdom of God. We must take back our own individual ministries and set right the government of the church.

It is much like our civil government that has gotten so big and powerful that "We the People" in this country is virtually non-existent today.

Let's not let this upside down church government overpower us any longer. Let us go back to the genuine New Testament way of doing church and show our Lord we can be trusted with the true priestly ministry of every believer. 1Cor 12 & 14.

I will tell you that even the Jews in their Synagogues had an open forum. They would allow anyone present to speak.

That is how Jesus, Paul and Peter as well as others could get up and share what they had to say. Even if it offended the Priests and the Pharisees they still had the opportunity to speak their mind.

The open forum is what we have lost in the Church. While a very few have the opportunity to share, everyone else sits quietly and idly watching whomever is on stage.

I am well aware there are times for apostolic teaching, vision and corporate celebration, but real true church and ministry is in the small group setting with everyone participating.

Chapter 11

Denominations

Denominations

The definition of denomination is division. A five dollar bill is "divided" from a one dollar bill. It is a different denomination than the others.

Paul even had this problem in the first century Church when some would say, "I am of Apollos, I am of Paul, or I am of Cephus".

Denominations occur when there is either disagreement or favoritism for and among the people. Neither of these reasons is healthy or biblical.

Denomination's set the Church against itself and creates confusion within and without the Church. They create suspicion, arguments and even war. The devil enjoys it when he can put lies in people's minds where one brother turns against another.

We always find ourselves asking, "What do you believe" as we determine if we want to fellowship with a certain brother or sister.

If a brother doesn't believe the same as we do on a certain pet doctrine then we automatically put up an invisible wall and limit any future contact with that person. It doesn't matter if they're a Christian or not.

We have concentrated so long on our differences that our similarities pale in comparison. The sad part being that Jesus expects us all to be "ONE" and yet we are not.

The fact that we both believe on the Lord Jesus Christ as our Savior and Lord becomes almost irrelevant in the face of Calvinism vs. Armenianism or tongues vs. no tongues etc.

Any one doctrine can set brothers and sisters at odds with each other quicker than anything we can think of and there are a myriad of them out there.

Sadly, the Church helps satan so that he doesn't have to work so hard because we're doing his job for him.

There are brothers and sisters all over the world that need our fellowship and our love. We must concentrate on the Lordship of Jesus and His love for the whole body rather than our petty differences.

Some may have lousy teachers who teach strange doctrines but if they believe on the Lord Jesus Christ as their Savior and Lord they are saved.

I believe that the Mormons' and Jehovah's Witnesses are basically cults, but within their ranks are a few true believers in Jesus. Just like in the Baptist denomination and even in the so called "Full Gospel" groups (of which I have been raised) there are people who believe and people who don't.

Whatever happened to "you will know them by their fruit" and "you will know them by their love"? And even further than that, what happened to "love your neighbor as yourself and love you enemies"?

Christians can divide over the smallest of issues quicker than anything else in their lives. It is a sad thing.

I may be a "Charismatic" or Pentecostal but the Baptist or Presbyterian is my brother and we are all made in His image and part of the same Kingdom of God.

Lord, help us to act like brothers and sisters without the sibling rivalry that separates us in our journey here on earth.

If we are commanded by our Lord to pray for those who despitefully use us then why can't we have good fellowship with those in the body who are brothers and sisters but may see things differently than we do?

In the last chapter I used 1Cor 12 & 14 several times to emphasize the need for complete body ministry. This chapter is all about 1Cor 13, the Love Chapter. The existence of Denominations proves that 1Cor 13 has been completely disregarded over and over throughout history.

Men, power and money have gotten in the way of the true Church that Jesus is building and yet His Church lives on. Pray that we may become one once again, as Jesus intended.

Pray that unity and love is the signature of the Church and that the world will take note of that powerful force.

Chapter 12

Traditions of Men

Traditions of Men

The word tradition comes from the Greek word paradosis meaning ordinance or precept.

Some traditions are good like birthdays or going to a favorite vacation spot, but when it comes to traditions in the church we need to examine and be careful about how they were originated.

In Matt 15:2-6 and Mk 7:3-13 Jesus talked about people holding to men's traditions rather than the commandments of God.

That is much like today. For instance, when we look into the Word of God and find out that we've been doing church by man's model all these many years, will we have the courage to change or stay with our traditions?

Men's traditions have ravaged the Church and its ability to operate in power, influence and effectiveness.

I look for the John the Baptists, or the Stephens who will stand up to men's traditions and say, NO MORE!

No more driving to church and sitting down and going through the motions on yet another Sunday like the good little Christian robots that we are.

You can say you like the reverence and the solemnity of a high church service, but what are you really getting out of it? Your spirit man is literally starving and you don't even know it. Your spiritual growth is stunted and your inner man hasn't been changed one bit.

We should be looking for anointing and passion, not tradition. Passion is like a river. Even if it is wrongly directed at least it gets you somewhere. Tradition is stagnant like a pond with no outlet it eventually will start to stink.

I can imagine the modern day John the Baptist appealing to the crowd, "Gosh guys, I sure wish you would come to Jesus. He'll take all your sins and make you prosperous, but if you'd rather not I don't want to offend anyone".

No more of that annoying "repent, for the Kingdom of heaven is at hand" stuff. After all we're not here to offend people and we want to be "relevant" in today's world.

I realize that the condemnation method was a man made approach and didn't do much for the kingdom. But we have certainly gone too far the other way by not challenging the world to repent from their sins and not discipling the believer to become grownup in Christ.

Courtesy and the "you are a winner" message have
replaced the whole counsel of God. We seem to leave off the part
that says, rejoice when men shall revile you and persecute you for
my sake, for great is your reward in heaven.

Instead we want our rewards right here, right now. I'm
sorry but the Word is very much different than what we hear from
the pulpit today. The conclusion is, let us re-examine our
traditions, asking "are they scriptural or not?" and do our best to
line up with the Word of God.

Chapter 13

Giving versus tithing

Giving versus Tithing

All my Christian life I've been taught to tithe and had no real objection to tithing.

Except for some occasional misguided motivational almost coercive speeches on tithing I had no problem with it. We were all taught to do our part because it was commanded in the Bible.

The problem though with tithing is that it is an old-testament principle not a new testament one.

The preacher would always have to go to Malachi to make his point on tithing, never the new -testament.

"Will you rob God?" would be the question. No self respecting Christian believer would ever want to rob God.

The trouble with tithing is that it is an old- testament command, although it is biblical in principle, it is still old testament.

The Word says that "God loves a cheerful giver" not a cheerful tither. Tithing is not giving, and giving is not based on commands.

Giving is based on free will, not coercion. It is a heart issue
and is a higher principle than tithing. Whether you give or tithe
begrudgingly you forfeit any reward you would have otherwise
had.

"For God so loved the world that He GAVE His only
begotten Son" Therefore we so love God that we are happy to give
into His Kingdom and to help those who have not.

In the modern American church it is unheard of what the
saints did in the book of Acts where the people sold everything that
they had and laid the proceeds at the apostle's feet. In the first
century church there was true, spontaneous and cheerful giving.

In America today we love our stuff too much to part with it,
even if it puts us in debt up to our eyeballs. The kingdom can wait,
the stuff is important.

If we were to sell all that we had and give it to the poor,
most people would think we were crazy or foolish or both.

On the subject of giving, I have a personal story to illustrate
how I view spontaneous cheerful giving.

Every year at Christmas time and when birthdays would
come around, my wife Juanita and I would always have a
discussion about giving.

She would say, "What if you got me something I didn't
want?" "Why don't you just let me pick out what I want and I'll be
happy"?

I would in turn tell her, "Honey, that's not giving, that's
called shopping." In my way of thinking, giving is something you
do for the other person when they don't expect, or even deserve the
gift.

You hope that they like and accept your gift, but sometimes
they don't. It's the same thing with God. Some people like and
accept His gift and some don't. That doesn't make the love behind
the gift any less valuable.

You GIVE because you LOVE. You GIVE because you
CARE. It is not a command or a mutually negotiated contract or
shopping. Giving is love operating when you don't expect anything
in return.

One year during Christmas Juanita and I could've given the
usual electronic, battery operated, made in China gifts, but we
decided something different that year.

We were going to make boxes for everyone in the family.
These were the kind that would resemble jewelry boxes.

I enjoy working with wood. So I found some ordinary
molding lumber you would normally trim out your house with and
got to work.

We were able to make 13 boxes. Juanita painted them and
put felt on the inside so they would look as much like jewelry
boxes as possible. They were beautiful.

To me, this was a gift made with my own two hands and made with love. It didn't matter if our children didn't like their gift. These were given from the heart not because of some tradition.

Tithing is so much more inferior to giving because it is tied to a command rather than to the free will of the giver. Also tithing has nothing to do with the heart; whereas a gift is completely motivated by the heart.

All these principles we are talking about go back to man's traditions and things we've been taught for centuries.

Some day I hope the Word of God will become important again to the body of Christ and more precious than other possessions so that we read it, study it, and digest it, rather than taking it for granted and trusting in men's traditions.

One last thought on giving; when we come to Christ and accept Him as our Savior and Lord; we no longer want to engage in sin, not because we are commanded but because we love Him so much that He is the only one we want to **give** ourselves to.

Chapter 14

Discipleship

Mathetes in Greek mean a learner, a pupil, a disciplined one. It is where we get our work discipline.

What is true discipleship? Is it a 14 week classroom course on how to be a better Christian? Is it the never ending preaching from the pulpit that makes one a disciple? Or is it a one-on-one, ongoing mentoring by a more mature Christian to develop the new believer into someone the devil is afraid of?

Jesus chose 12 men to be His disciples. How did He train and raise up these 12 uneducated and at times unruly men? Did He teach in the classroom or preach from the pulpit?

Jesus taught with multiple methods but not in a classroom setting. He taught His disciples as they went through life; on the road, on the hillside, and anywhere He could and yes even in the synagogue.

But more than teaching, Jesus knew these men intimately. He knew their strengths and their weaknesses, their likes and dislikes. He was not a distant instructor with any intimate contact with His students.

Jesus knew every man's own individual personality. He knew the spiritual gifts which God had given them. He was much more than their teacher, He was their brother, and He was family.

In today's churches, all too often you can go to class week after week and nobody knows your name and nobody knows anything about you.

You are just another friendly face in the crowd for two hours on Sunday and then forgotten the rest of the week. I know that some would say, "not my church", but all too often this is the case.

It is not a new or unusual phenomenon. Millions of people all over this country and around the world who are in traditional churches depending on classroom type teaching to do the job of discipleship are falling short and stunting the spiritual growth of new believers.

Sometimes you start to wonder if it's all about their ministry, their status, their church and less about you and the Kingdom of God.

Without intimate discipleship people go hungry for fellowship in the Word and some type of real spiritual connection with the church body.

And even if there is fellowship there is a lack of discipleship on the part of the churches when they are not mentoring new believers, but instead depending on teachings that are not applied in real world situations.

Jesus not only taught the Word but He demonstrated the Word with power and occasionally sent His disciples out on their own to practice what they had learned with real world application.

With Jesus there was always a hands-on training of His pupils.

In the modern church I realize that people live busy lives and don't have the time to train or be trained as intimately as Jesus did with His disciples. At least that is the excuse in many cases.

Why can't there be elders all over the church to disciple young Christians since they are already taking the time to prepare for their classes. I am not only referring to a youth pastor, I am talking about all available mature Christians mentoring and teaching and applying all that they know. Youth ministry is one thing, with its games and activities but discipleship is quite another.

If we want people to grow up in the Lord spiritually there has to be some priorities set and some time taken. Let's take the time to disciple the new believers and see our rewards come rolling in.

After all, we are trying to raise spiritual children to maturity to be able to withstand the wiles of the devil in real life situations. And if we are sincere about discipleship, there must be a greater effort on the part of the leadership in the church to do so.

If you look around you will find a generation of people who have been in the church for decades but who are baby Christians nonetheless.

They were not discipled but rather put on the rolls as now being "Christian" and must "conform" or "fit" to the way we do things. As a result you wind up with people in their 60's and 70's that are spiritually weak.

So when adversity comes their natural tendency is to seek out someone to pray for them or for counseling, because they don't have enough spiritual strength to take on the devil by themselves.

Discipleship should take only a few years and not decades. Although we are ever learning and growing in the Word, we as teachers should be like the eagle that properly trains the eaglet then pushes the eaglet out of the nest to face life for itself and make room for another generation.

But if you don't have proper discipleship in place, the next generation of ministers are not available for ministry on their own. They are, instead having to be continually ministered to because of the lack of discipleship.

It is my contention that if a child is properly discipled in the Word, by the time he is old enough for seminary he should be able to teach the class. I am referring strictly to the Bible not the extra courses they offer to get a degree as a future pastor.

I say then, because many remain weak spiritually, and because we are responsible to them and to God we will answer for that shortfall, or at least be deprived of any reward that we thought we might otherwise receive.

Make no mistake; satan has his own discipleship program going on in a myriad of false religions and secularism.

Think of the religions of the world and their indoctrination. Think of the anti Christ secular sentiments in our country alone which daily are embellished and supported by television, radio, and classroom training.

The world is doing its job discipling. Where is the Church? We are, to say the least, behind the curve on this front, because we have not taken DISCIPLESHIP seriously.

Sermons can only do so much and pastors need to wake up and utilize every gift and calling within the local body before there is yet another generation of lethargic, liturgical church goers who are, Christians in name only.

If we believe we are living in the last days, we have an enormous responsibility to prepare those who will be facing a very hostile world and an enemy who has come to kill, steal and destroy.

In reality a disciple should be fully equipped for all and any spiritual battle within a couple or three years not 3, 4, or 5 decades or more.

"Do nothing" Christians are of little value in the Kingdom of God and absolutely no threat to the devil. Discipleship must take place and fruit must be produced.

Below is an actual "discipleship" program by a very
popular church in the United States. I will not use the name of the
church or the pastor, but simply share their concept of what they
call discipleship.

Discipleship 102 "Becoming a disciple of Jesus Christ"

• Attend a 12-week discipleship cell group

"Growing in Christ"
•Read the Bible daily
•Daily Prayer
•Attend Church on a regular Basis
•Share Your Faith
•Tithe
•Attend an Encounter Weekend

At the end of the 12 weeks you will receive a certificate of
completion

Discipleship 201 "Becoming a Disciple Maker"

•Attend or listen to DVDs on the Foundation Class
•Fill out and turn in the Servant Leader application
•Attend Classes specific to Men and to Women
•Attend a Cell Leader Orientation
•Attend the Personality Profile training
•Begin to apprentice in a connect group of your choice
•After the apprenticeship begin to lead your own group

I will let you be the judge of whether you believe this is Biblical discipleship or something else.

I am not denying that prayer and reading your Bible daily helps in making disciples, but there was much more to what Jesus and Paul and others did to "disciple" new believers than the formerly mentioned method.

I see nothing in the above illustration of a one on one relationship with anyone. It's all centered on classroom curriculum and an almost assembly line efficiency.

These methods could easily be used by any corporation in the world. Notice words like application and apprentice and then you get a certificate of completion.

Our methods in the Church have become so professionalized and clinical that it has ceased to be a living, "organic" and natural "Body" of believers.

In Jesus own words, what has He commanded us to do?

Matthew 28:18 All power is given unto me in heaven and in earth. Go therefore and teach all nations, baptizing then in the name of the Father, and of the Son, and of the Holy Ghost; Teaching them to observe all things whatsoever I have commanded you; and lo, I am with you always, even unto the end of the world.

Mark 16:15 Go ye into all the world and preach the gospel to every creature. He that believes shall be saved; but he that believes not shall be damned. And these signs shall follow them that believe; in my name shall they cast out devils; they shall speak with new tongues; they shall take up serpents; and if they drink any deadly thing, it shall not hurt them; they shall lay hands on the sick and they shall recover.

Luke 24:47 and that repentance and remission of sins should be preached in His name among all nations, beginning in Jerusalem. And you are witnesses of these things. And, behold, I send the promise of my Father upon you; but wait in the city of Jerusalem until you are endued with power from on high.

Acts 1:8 but you shall receive power after the Holy Ghost has come upon you; and you shall be witnesses unto me both in Jerusalem and in all Judaea and in Samaria and unto the uttermost part of the earth.

I see nothing in there about 12 week classes or connect groups. And there is nothing in the Word about certificates of completion or filling out applications.

Please, I pray that the Church wakes up, and revives and sees what it has done to itself. It truly is a shadow of its former self; a mere skeleton of the original.

I must add that these are good, well intentioned people who love the Lord and would not do anything to dishonor His name. But the above mentioned program is hardly Biblical and falls short in discipleship. It is a direct result of the pastor led corporation style church that is more efficient than it is spiritually sound.

Chapter 15

Raising up and sending out

Raising up and sending out is a hot button of mine. It is a continuation of principles set forth by discipleship. Are we in the ministry, or are we operating a business where numbers and money mean much more than the souls of people?

I believe in true discipleship. I also believe that every local church of any size should have its own Bible school or training center. The Bible school should exist not to turn a profit, but to turn out ministers of the Gospel and not just pastors.

I am truly tired of seeing people who have been Christians for decades that need to be fed milk all the time.

It is the fault of the leadership in the body of Christ. They enable people and keep them perpetually in the spiritual baby stage so that when any little crisis in their lives comes their way they either fall apart or have to run to the pastor for help. They are constantly dependent upon him.

That creates great job security for the pastor, but it doesn't do much for the body. It doesn't do much in the way of "equipping the saints" for the work of the ministry Eph 4:11.

Pastors who do not train their people in the Word and depend solely on sermons on Sunday morning are much like one group of people who want you completely dependent on them. These people are number one enablers.

Let's keep the masses dependent on us. That way we will
retain our power and prestige. On the other hand an apostle is
much like another group who wants you to become self sufficient
with more freedom and responsibility.

I wonder what the Church would be like if each local body
had a Stephen, or a couple of John the Baptists, or several Paul's
and Peters.

What is the difference? We say we're filled with the Spirit
and that we have the gifts and fruit of the Spirit. What makes us so
different from the 1st Century Church? Are we truly filled or are
we deceiving ourselves?

If we are filled with the Spirit, then could it be the lack of
proper training in the Word or the lack of true discipleship?

In my view, I believe it is both. First of all when you have
pastors doing the entire work of the ministry, this is a system that
automatically stunts the growth of the body of Christ. Those who
are supposed to be equipped to do the work of the ministry are
prevented from doing so because of that system.

If a parent carries its newborn child everywhere it goes
until that child is grown the child will be unable to walk on its own
because of the atrophy of their muscles.

In the short run, the child enjoys the convenience of not
falling and not having to exert much energy, but in the long run,
the child's growth is stunted to the point of being crippled by its
own loving, but enabling parent.

The Church, in its structure is actually committing the same
atrocities against its own people by stunting their spiritual growth
and doing the "ministry" for them instead of equipping them to
stand on their own.

I realize it all is unintentional and we feel we are operating
in love. But the fact remains, if you do everything for a person they
will never become strong responsible and healthy human beings, or
in this case believers.

Another example would be if a parent did their child's
homework for them instead of challenging them to think for
themselves. You get the same results, absolute stunted growth, and
low SAT scores.

For centuries the elitists in the Roman Catholic church and
then later in the Protestant church literally kept the Word of God
out of the hands of the common people.

William Tyndale was actually burned at the stake for
translating the Bible into English and then teaching his students the
Word in their own common language.

It is much the same way today, although not as drastic as
martyrdom, but nonetheless the subtleness of withholding the
Word still exists.

The fact that you have one person doing the ministry
hinders the growth of everyone else in the congregation, because
they become dependent and apathetic. They have no motivation to
learn and study and travail over the Word for themselves because
they have someone else to do it for them.

Pastors you need to please, MOVE OVER, AND MAKE
ROOM FOR THE REST OF US.

I ask the pastor, is your job security more important than
the Kingdom of God? Is it more important than the spiritual
growth and well being of the Body of Christ?

There are many pastors out there who micro manage the
church that they have been entrusted with. In reality they are
stunting the spiritual maturity of their friends and loved ones in
that body.

If you are micro managing, realize that it is a form of fear.
It's fear because you can't let go and trust others with the ministry.
And we all know that fear is the opposite of faith.

You don't need to preside over every Bible study and
prayer group.

Think of it this way; if you are such a good Bible teacher and great example to the people, then shouldn't you have confidence that your training will carry them through many of the trials of life?

Shouldn't the more mature Christians be able to teach the newer believers without you hovering over them?

What needs to take place is, that leaders need to teach the people to be self sufficient to where if something were to happen to the leadership, then the church carries on without being put into a panic.

No one in the church should be indispensible, although there obviously needs to be some time for transition, but not an entire shut down or a call for another leader to come from far away to rescue this poor church.

The local body should have several leaders (elders and presbyters) to step in at a moment's notice; in fact they should already be ministering to the body in the first place.

The local church should always be raising up new ministers on a continuous basis and then releasing them into their own ministry.

Some may stay to build up that body with their gifts and some may feel called to other locations, which brings me to another point concerning mega churches.

Understand I have nothing against mega churches, but is there no one in that body of literally thousands able to carry on their own ministry elsewhere? How is it that people stay with one man and one church until they become a small city?

It is my contention that we must not only raise up but send out workers, ministers, apostles and so forth to effectively take ground back from the enemy.

We must train those coming up to enter the battlefield equipped and ready to have an answer that lies within them.

We in this country especially have become social Christians where you must realize the enemy of the faith is not sociable at all. He is out to kill, steal and destroy and "Club Christian" needs to arm itself with the Word and not self help sermons.

I charge pastors to look at the folly of the last 1700 plus years and read books like Pagan Christianity and The Reformation of the Glorious Church and start making room for the intense equipping of the Saints.

The word repent comes to mind. It means to change direction or to change your mind. Pastor, you are one of the keys to raising up and sending people out.

The Church that Jesus wants to build is not our empire or job security until retirement. It is to be a powerful force on the earth, taking ground from the devil at every turn.

The Church is to be a great influence on this world and not the other way around. Jesus said, "my kingdom is not of this world."

We are also so afraid of offending anyone that we are completely ineffective as a Church. While the world infiltrates the Church and puts its own demands on it, we on the other hand go out of our way trying not to offend people as we compromise our principles.

I will refer back to the beginning of this book. Jesus didn't set out to offend those around Him, but if they were offended He didn't apologize for it.

Jesus said that the Word of God will offend people, so why do we, as the Church, walk on egg shells and let the world dictate to us what we should say or do?

If people are offended by the preaching or practicing of the Gospel, I say, that's too bad, but let's carry on and do what God has commanded us to do.

Let us equip and send then equip and send again. I hope we don't need another 9-11 to wake us up. Lord, revive us today so that we do not need calamity to open our eyes. Have mercy on us as we repent and choose the better way, your way.

EQUIP, EQUIP, EQUIP and then push them out of the nest so they can fly.

Chapter 16

The Mega-Church

How big is too big

The Mega Church

I certainly have mixed feelings about mega churches. As I stated in the last chapter I don't necessarily have anything against mega-churches per se. But how is it that you can have a congregation of 5,000 or 10,000 people or more and no one wants to leave that large congregation to start their own ministry? What are their motives for staying? Is it because of one man and his charisma or is it because they feel the kingdom is better served?

This can only be answered by the individual. Although I do believe it is up to the leadership to make that observation public. Of course in an elder led congregation you have less of an opportunity for "idol" worship of a single individual.

I know we have jobs and homes and family and we want to put down roots and not wander. But within such a large community of believers where are the people that have the calling to open up new fields of ministry?

Yes, the Mega Church has resources that can accomplish many great things in and for the Kingdom of God that seemingly the small group cannot, such as media ministry and foreign missions. As long as that church is reaching out beyond their 4 walls and not plowing the same ground over and over it can be an effective ministry for the kingdom.

I understand that Jesus had multitudes following Him, otherwise how would He have fed the 5,000. I also realize there are more followers than there are leaders.

But once you have heard the gospel and accepted Jesus and then you are discipled to maturity, what is the next step. Don't you have a responsibility to share what you have learned and received from the Lord? Or will you stay and listen to the same sermons year after year by the same person.

Is there something in you that needs to come out? Is there a message, a calling, an unction that needs an outlet? What are you called to do?

Are you or are you not being recognized in your own ministry? Have you been encouraged to step out and fulfill your vision? Or has there been opposition, delay or even a deaf ear to that calling?

I'm not saying to step out there ahead of God's timing, but has God given you the go ahead and the church's leadership throws a wet blanket on your vision?

Sometimes that is how a mega church is built. There is a sense that you are not ready yet, so stay here awhile longer and "wait and wait and wait" on the Lord.

So then you have thousands of people waiting on the Lord on the sidelines and in the meantime the church grows larger and larger as you "submit to their authority" and their vision.

All the while, with the church expanding, they start another building program and take up extra offerings and pledges to fulfill their needs.

I know this sounds very negative, but in reality it's not too far-fetched to at least make the observation. What I'm saying is, are you really supposed to stay? Is this truly what God wants you to do or have you been called out by the Lord?

Don't let the security of having a church to go to every Sunday influence your decision. The only thing you need to consider is, did God tell me to do this or not?

If the answer is stay, then stay, simple as that. But I have seen too many people that have been called out and try to seek the approval of church leadership and never get it.

Meanwhile, someone else has to take their place because God is trying to fill in a gap and they're not there to do their part.

There is another subject about mega churches that I don't understand. Why are there no small groups or house churches in some of them? They have the resources to establish house churches all over the city but never do so.

Where is spiritual growth coming from? Is it the pulpit? That's very one dimensional and near sighted on the part of the leadership. And frankly I see it as rather arrogant on the part of the preacher, as if he's the only one that can teach, counsel or pray for the people.

What is their goal? What are they trying to accomplish with having such a large congregation and no extra or outside ministry or fellowship or training?

We in the Christian Church love to use metaphors. Ask yourself this question. Is my church a mill or factory or is it a warehouse or storeroom?

Mills and factories produce something which goes to market and there is visible movement and use of that product. A warehouse is a place where objects sit and gather dust.

Every church is different. Which is yours? Is your church producing strong ministers of the Gospel or are they keeping the sheep in the pen, fat and contented?

Chapter 17

Celebrity

"Ministers"

I am aware that Jesus himself was a celebrity. He had thousands of people following Him. Also Peter and Paul had their share of large crowds and people who wanted to put them on pedestals.

Regrettably many of Jesus' followers were only there to seek after a sign. They were there to watch the miracles and see demons cast out. They were there to watch the show. But when things got tough for their leader they abandoned Him.

Celebrity ministers today are basically treated like rock stars. They have their own entourage with security guards and all of the fanfare that goes with it.

We must be careful how the big named minister is perceived and celebrated, first of all for our sakes and secondly for theirs.

The only difference between the local minister and the celebrity is the amount of people who know them. The well known preacher/teacher is no more called, no more knowledgeable, and no more consecrated to the Word than the local minister.

There are many dangers connected with being a famous preacher. They are no different than the movie star, the professional athlete, or singer. All of these are people with human weaknesses and desires, like notoriety, money and temptation at every turn.

Pride is a constant enemy that lurks in every passageway. In fact, pride is probably the greatest enemy of all.

Adoration can corrupt and cripple a person spiritually in a greater way than rejection can. Proverbs 16:18 Pride goes before destruction and a haughty spirit before a fall. Verse 19 Better is it to be of a humble spirit with the lowly, than to divide the spoil with the proud.

For the last 30 years or so we have been hearing messages like, "you are the righteousness of God in Christ Jesus", and "Something good is about to happen to you" and, "we are kings and priests."

All these messages are good and scriptural in themselves because there needed to be a counter balance to "you're a sinner and going to hell" or "I'm just an old sinner saved by grace" message.

In that period of time there has been a lack of messages on humility. A sense of false pride has crept in the Church and become a dominating factor. A balance must be struck between knowing who you are in Christ and He sees you as righteous and the message that reminds us that it is His righteousness and not our own.

False humility is still pride. We should no more be raked over the coals than we are to be coroneted.

Those who are on television have a great opportunity with a larger audience and a lot of resources, but there is also great responsibility to tell the truth and the whole story, while at the same time keeping himself/or herself up-spotted from the world.

Remember the story in Acts 14 where the people called Barnabas, Jupiter, and they called Paul; Mercury. Their fame could have gotten them in big trouble with the Lord, but fortunately they handled themselves well.

At the same time, let us not be like that crowd and make certain ones more than what they are; ministers and servants of the Lord God.

I admit I have been bothered by some things I've seen and heard on TV and radio, but my job is to pray for them and believe in God's correction.

Besides, how well would I be able to handle fame and fortune and all that adulation? Apparently not very well since God has not entrusted me with those things.

Celebrity ministers; there's nothing wrong with it, but they must keep their message Biblical and their hearts right with God not being puffed up. Frankly speaking, that is between them and the Lord.

Chapter 18

Salaries and Mortgages

Salaries and Mortgages

I have actually sat in million dollar pieces of church property with 12 people sitting in the pews on Sunday morning. WHY?

We would suppose to commend the pastor and the 12 followers for their faithfulness and commitment, but what are they really committed to?

Is it to the pastor, to God or is it that building and property? Don't we have an obligation to the kingdom of God to re examine our motives and our stewardship of what the Lord has entrusted us with?

The pastors salary and the church mortgage is sometimes like a stone around the neck of those who are left in that congregation and then coerced into "tithing" to keep this thing they call a church, afloat.

Sometimes there are 2 or 3 people in the church that can pay the bills and sustain it, but why put the burden on them? And why give them the temptation of having to call the shots because they financially have control of the church?

Is this good stewardship? Is this freedom? Is the pastor now obligated to preach only what these people want to hear?

What is the point in hanging onto a piece of property when there is no way to support it? It's like that show, where the guy has a plant that feeds on flesh and it's always demanding to the guy, "Feed Me" until one day I think it eats him.

Shouldn't that body find themselves a buyer for the property and then find a living room for the people so they can have church like they did in the New Testament?

Wisdom needs to be exercised. When you are drowning in debt, get out of the pool.

We like using a phrase; Where God guides, He will provide". If down the road you find yourself without provision, doesn't that saying still hold true?

Additionally, what is the real motive for taking up the offering? Is it to worship the Lord with our giving and help those in need or is it "I hope there's enough to pay the light bill and my salary?" This is not a new message. Desperation out of debt can make people do strange things. I know this first hand.

And how can you be loyal to an inanimate object like a building any way? Your house is a building, a library is a building, and a grocery store is a building.

If you move into one of venues previously mentioned there could be great things happen in the Spirit that you never dreamed possible. That is, if you unload the burden of a church property that you cannot maintain.

God can finally work with a group of believers that aren't constantly fixated on brick and mortar.

Your individual situation might not be as drastic as what is described above but it wouldn't hurt to re evaluate our motives.

As far as the subject of the pastors salary; whether the church is struggling or whether they have millions, a question should be asked, "Would the pastor continue in the ministry if that monetary provision were removed forever?

If that minister knew he would have to live in a grass hut or be chased by persecutors the rest of his life, would he still be a preacher of the gospel?

I think that is a good, honest question we all need to ponder on a regular basis. Looking inside and alone before God asking "Am I a hireling or am I not?"

Paul the apostle was a tent maker. He did not have a salary from any of the churches he founded. In fact, he had an aversion to it. Instead he would take up offerings for other struggling churches, such as the one in Jerusalem.

Paul's provision either came from working with his own two hands or God providing some other way and yes, possibly offerings from time to time, but he didn't have a guaranteed salary, a pension plan and a 401k. Trusting God was his guarantee.

I cannot examine a person's motives except to exhort them to look into their own heart and discuss the matter with their Heavenly Father.

The same is true for me. Am I writing this book to make lots of money and receive notoriety or do I feel that I have a message that needs to be told and this might be my best and only platform? That question is between me and my Lord.

Chapter 19

A Church of Spectators

A Church of Spectators

For 1700 years the Church as a whole has become filled with spectator Christians, people who do nothing more than sit and sing songs, listen to sermons and give in the offering and sit some more.

In other words, the Church as a whole has become passive, inert, ineffective and inept. That is what the one man rule within the Church has caused.

Satan has also for 1700 paralyzed the church by making the believers watchers of ministry rather than doers of ministry. The result has been weak, selfish, baby Christians, who if they don't get their way can run off to another church and sit there and watch.

Maybe it's just me, but I can't just sit and watch someone else minister to people year after year and not get involved myself. I know I have been called and I know there is something for me to do and I know that daily there are many opportunities for me to be used of God.

I cannot be a spectator. If the opportunities are not in the big church setting or I am not approved by man in their system, I still have a job to do for God.

Whether this book accomplishes what I hope or not, I still have been given the task of writing it and believing God for what He does with it.

I like watching football on TV because I can't play it anymore, but when it comes to the ministry I refuse to be a spectator on the sidelines, watching someone else, sitting idle and refusing to get involved. My goal is to be actively involved in ministry until someone carries me to my final resting place.

With all of the sermons that we hear and all of the lessons etc., what are we suppose to do with that? Is it all just for our own comfort? Is it there so we can stroke our own conscience and feel good about ourselves? Or are we supposed to actually do something with what we've learned?

When I hear a message from the Word of God, I think of how I can apply it in my life. What is the life lesson and how can someone else benefit from this lesson?

Christianity is not a spectator event. It is not only there for our comfort. It is who we are and what we are. Our Christian lives are to be lived out and shared with others. We, the body of Christ, are all ministers of the Gospel. Jesus commanded, "Go and make disciples."

I feel that spectator Christianity is a crime against the Kingdom of God because IF YOU'RE NOT TAKING GROUND FOR GOD YOU MUST BE HOLDING GROUND FOR THE DEVIL.

Being a sitter in the Church is ultra boring to me. Why even go to church if there is nothing to contribute or share.

I am a part of the Body of Christ, a minister of the Word of God, not a piece of furniture. If I can't contribute or if I am not allowed to, I go my way to where my gifts are celebrated and used.

I know there are people who prefer to sit and do nothing, but I also know people who hunger for the day when their ministry will be recognized. God recognizes your ministry, He gave it to you.

Shame on the pastors who perpetuate the one man, professionals only type church. You are actually standing in the way of God's plan and purposes.

You as pastor say you want more people to get involved in the church, then why don't you recognize them for who they are, ministers of God and your spiritual equals.

The pastor actually creates the spectator problem, with the governmental system they operate in. There is no room for ministry, except for the professionals. It's a contradictory and counterproductive system.

If you want to sit up here on the platform in these nice embroidered chairs, you go to college and seminary, get you degree and your license and ordination then we'll give you permission to speak.

No wonder people sit there and do nothing. Tell me what does a license or ordination and all that stuff have to do with receiving a revelation from God? What does it have to do with having a burden for lost souls or teaching?

Peter, James, and John didn't get a certificate before they were qualified to preach the Gospel. Neither did Barnabas, or Silas or even Jesus for that matter.

Only Paul comes closest to the scenario of possessing man-made qualifications. He was a Pharisee and highly educated in men's traditions yet after finding the Lord in his life he considered those things to be of less value than the spirit of God.

You people who are sitting in the pews; I am talking directly to you now. If God told you to start a Bible study in your home, then start it. If you get the blessing from the leadership, fine. If not, start it anyway. You must follow what God has told you over that of man. Also remember that the professionals don't have all the answers and they are not perfect.

Brother and sister; get out of your seats or pews and do what God has called you to do. Don't wait for permission from men. You might be waiting a very long time.

One last thing, you recall that when Jesus was crucified that
the veil was torn in two. That means God has given us all access to
Him, not only concerning prayer but also ministry.

Don't allow a pastor, or staff member or anyone else get
between you and your ministry. In Jesus' time it was the
priesthood and the Pharisees. Today it's pastors and other
leadership in the church.

Go ahead and step through that invisible barrier into your
own priesthood with boldness, knowing you are highly favored of
the Lord and have His approval, regardless of what man says.

Chapter 20

Words and Terms we use today

Words and Terms we use today

These are just a few and I am sure we all can add to the list of terms that we use in the modern church that cannot be found in the Bible.

Clergy

According to George Barna and frank Viola in their book "Pagan Christianity" pg 113 "Tertullion was the first writer to use the word clergy to refer to a separate class of Christians. Those who were qualified to do ministry and those who were not.

Reverend

Are we to reverence men or God? To me, the man or woman who puts reverend on their business card and stationary is a bit arrogant and should read again the scriptures on humility. I myself have been called reverend, but I don't like it because I am not to be put in any position of reverence.

Man of the Cloth

I'm truly curious about this one. What cloth are they referring to? Where did this term originate anyway?

Slain in the Spirit

I've been in many Pentecostal churches and witnessed a lot of strange things. One is being "slain in the Spirit". I never could understand the purpose and I can't find it anywhere in the Bible. Are we simply trying to help God by being a little spooky at times. My friends will be unhappy with me on this one, but I am simply trying to figure out the biblical need for these actions and teachings.

Layman

The word lay or layman means ignorant, to put down, beat down, to place in a lying down position or a position of rest, to put in place, in orderly fashion, to impose a burden or penalty, to make quiet, to make disappear, to lay to waste. Have you been put in your place, put down and been made quiet. That seems to be what has happened to most people in the Church. Besides if there is a lay pastor in the congregation, I would hesitate to use someone who is ignorant and doesn't know what he is doing, which is what the word "lay" implies.

Rector

Not found in the Bible

The Pew

Not found in the Bible

"Holy Laughter"

Not found in the Bible

Para-church ministry

Not found in the Bible. In fact, ministry is ministry wherever you find it. Para-church ministry implies that it is less important than the pastoral type ministry or what is going on at the big church building. Some people aren't bothered by the term, but I see it as a bit condescending.

The 501c3 Non Profit

Not found in the Bible. Jesus paid His taxes. In fact He told the people to render unto Caesar that which was Caesar's and render unto God that which was God's. He never used write-offs.

Crusade

If you ever want to witness to a Muslim, never use the word Crusade. To them it is a word that they equate with battles and suffering. It was a word that was synonymous with war against their people hundreds of years ago, but it is still fresh in their minds today. Besides it is not a Biblical word anyway.

Licensing

Not found in the Bible. Of course it was the Pharisees and other hypocrites that asked the question, "by what authority do you do these things?" That might tell us something about licensing and degrees and man-made qualifications. I am not against having an education but I am against anything that is a substitute for the Spirit of God.

What other terminology do we use today that is not found in the Bible? I am sure that you too can come up with your own terms that are manmade and unbiblical.

I would like to hear from you about your own list. Please feel free to send me all of your entries. I think we all would be fascinated to find so many words and practices that we use as Christians that are not Biblical or even found in the Word of God.

Chapter 21

The Rabbi

Duplicate Me

The Rabbi

Duplicate Me

In these next few paragraphs I must give credit to a minister by the name of Lance Walnau. This was just a small part of a lesson he taught one day at a conference I attended, but a lesson that bears repeating because I got a complete revelation of what Jesus was trying to do in the lives of the 12 disciples.

Brother Walnau stated that the reason why Peter got out of the boat when he saw Jesus walking on the water was because he saw the Rabbi doing it. The Rabbi's job is to duplicate himself. He is not only supposed to teach principles and give practical illustrations and lessons, but he is also there to turn that disciple or student into what he is. He is literally making a carbon copy of himself in the disciple.

Jesus as the Rabbi healed the sick, raised the dead and cast out demons. Then He required the 12 disciples to do the same. That commission has not changed for us today.

Matthew 28:18-20 All power is given unto me in heaven and in earth. Go therefore and teach all nations, baptizing them in the name of the Father, and the Son, and the Holy Ghost; teaching them to observe all things which I have commanded you and lo I am with you always, even to the end of the world.

Mark 16:17-18 These signs shall follow them that believe; In my name they shall cast out devils, they shall speak with new tongues; they shall take up serpents, and if they drink any deadly thing it shall not hurt them; they shall lay hands on the sick and the shall recover.

Our Rabbi, our Lord, expects us to do these things, because He was our example and He did these things as a man, not as God.

Remember that Jesus emptied Himself of all His Godly glory and power and came to earth as a man, a man that kept His relationship with God the Father so open that as a man He was able to perform these miracles.

Now, He as a man and a teacher expected His disciples to do what He did, and He expects the same of us. Jesus gave us the gift of the Holy Spirit for that empowerment, along with being our Comforter and Teacher.

He said all power was given unto Him by the Father, and He said He could do nothing except the Father tell Him. This means that Jesus was completely powerless without the Father.

It is truly sad that throughout history people have separated themselves from the MAN Jesus since He was God in the flesh and did all those miracles and died for our sins. How can we possibly do what He did? The answer is; because He gave us the power and the commandment to do so.

Our Lord, our Rabbi is trying to duplicate Himself in us and we fail because of our false concept of Jesus. He has been waiting for us to take our rightful place as His disciples and emulate Him.

Granted, we cannot die on the cross or any other way for anyone else's sins. That was His mission, but in every other way we are to be as He was and do as He did.

He is in truth trying to duplicate Himself in us and we have resisted Him for centuries. Maybe it's time we surrender to His will and step into our rightful place as His disciples and the Rabbis for a new generation.

I am excited about the future and the changes that will take place in the Church and in people's hearts as they discover the New Testament way of being the Church.

Chapter 22

Priests

Priests

The definition of priest is from the Greek word in Strong's Concordance, hiereus, which is pronounced, hee-er-yooce, meaning a priest. It's a simple definition, but very profound. It comes for the word, hieros, pronounced hee-er-os, which means sacred or holy.

Hebrews 3:1 Wherefore holy brethren, partakers of the heavenly calling, consider the Apostle and High Priest of our profession, Christ Jesus.

Hebrews 4:14,15,16 Seeing then that we have a great high priest that is passed into the heavens, Jesus the Son of God, let us hold fast our profession.

Vs 15 For we have not a high priest which cannot be touched with the feeling of our infirmities: but was in all points tempted like as we are, yet without sin.

Vs 16 Let us therefore come boldly into the throne of grace that we may obtain mercy and find grace to help in time of need.

So now, we have established that Jesus is our High Priest, but more than that, He has also made us the Body of Christ, priests as well.

Peter also establishes that we too are priests. Starting at 1 Peter 2:3 If so you have tasted that the Lord is gracious. To whom coming as onto a living stone, disallowed indeed of men but chosen of God, and precious. You also, as lively stones, are built up a spiritual house, a holy priesthood, TO OFFER UP SPIRITUAL SACRIFICES ACCEPTABLE TO GOD by Jesus Christ. This is the priesthood of the believer.

Do you see that? Peter says, that we are priests and that we are able to offer up spiritual sacrifices, acceptable to God.

In the Old Testament only the high priest was allowed to offer those sacrifices to God and to enter into the Holy of Holies.

That was all changed when Jesus was crucified. Remember the veil in the Temple was torn in two, giving all of us, as priests full access to offer up spiritual sacrifices.

So, why is there a priest or a pastor standing between you and God? Why are they considered to be in the ministry and you are not?

How is it then, in the Church we have allowed ourselves to go back to the Old Testament and fall into the Mosaic way of worshipping and serving God?

Jesus abolished the one-man rulership over the ministry. God ripped open the veil and gave all Christians access. In addition, he says to come boldly to the throne of grace.

Catholic priests and Protestant pastors have reversed what Jesus did on the cross by stepping in the way and blocking your access to the Father. It may not in prayer, but in your priesthood.

I realize that many of us know this whole concept concerning prayer, but it also has to do with ministry. That is why in Ephesians 4:11 he gave gifts unto men, so all believers are equipped for their own priesthood and ministry.

This does not mean a select few, but the entire body of Christ, which also means that you are just as qualified to do ministry as any minister, pastor, or priest.

Revelation 1:5-6… Jesus Christ, who is the faithful witness, and the first begotten of the dead, and the Prince of the kings of the earth. Unto Him that loved us and washed us from our sins in His own blood and has made us kings and priests unto God and His Father; to Him be glory and dominion forever and ever. Amen.

Notice verse 16. Let "US" therefore come boldly into the throne of grace that we may obtain mercy and find grace to help in time of need.

These scriptures are proof that the one-man, pastor, or priest system is not of God. It also proves that we all are priests before God and that was His plan in addition to our salvation. In fact, I contend that the two are inexplicably tied together.

Chapter 23

The Traditional Church

The Traditional Church

Being charismatic, I have attended church for decades, and one thing that the charismatic community has done is labeled certain other churches as "traditional".

A Methodist or Presbyterian church would be considered traditional. In addition, the Baptists, Adventists, Episcopalians and every other church that doesn't recognize the gifts of the Spirit and speaking in tongues.

But in reality, the charismatic community is as much a traditional entity as any other church. They still operate with a pastoral government, such as senior pastor, assistant pastor, and an order of service and most of all the formalities that make up the so called traditional church.

Committees and councils are also used in some charismatic churches. So, what makes them different from what they call traditional churches? I submit the answer is, not much at all.

What traditional church is basically a formalized body with ceremony, structure and order which has replaced a living, breathing "family of believers". What Frank Viola calls, "Organic Church".

The traditional church is run more like a business, than a church, in fact, they are a corporation. When you ask most churches about contributions to that ministry, they will tell you that your giving is tax deductable. Why is it tax deductible? They will tell you it is because the church is a 501c3 corporation.

I realize I am repeating myself but may I remind you that Jesus paid His taxes. He told His disciples to render unto Caesar that which is Caesar's and render unto God that which is God's. Matthew 22:21.

He did not have a tax deductable corporation. And the fact that your church has a tax deduction makes it a government approved and state sanctioned corporation.

Now, since your church is state sanctioned, how much power do they have over that church? The one obvious answer is that the church cannot endorse any political candidate using the threat of removing your tax deductable status.

But how much more power does the government have over your local church? My answer is, if they have any that is too much. Remember, we are in the world but not of it. And corporations, church or otherwise are of the world.

I say, come out from among them and be separate. We know we don't need the world's approval and that includes our own government.

I have a question for you. At which point would you give up your tax deductible status? How bad would our government and its controls have to be before you say "we are compromising our principles for a tax deduction and we refuse to continue on this path?"

I realize I raise a lot of questions, but I believe it is necessary to do so in the light of the scriptures.

Chapter 24

Covering

Covering

My late wife and I had ministered for many decades, and in many capacities and our combined ministry effort's equals over 82 years.

When we started a church in Granbury, Texas, one question that several pastors would ask us is; "who is your covering?" In other words what other pastor or ministry is keeping an eye on you to make sure you do everything right.

I was shocked. As if God wasn't enough. I would tell them that God was my covering and that I was responsible to the people that I ministered to.

My question to them was always, who is keeping an eye on the guy who was supposed to be the covering for their ministries? And then who was keeping an eye on them, and so on?

My covering has always been God, the Father. He is the one that I answer to, and if need be, the rest of the body of Christ.

I would think to myself what makes that other guy so special, so pure, and so full of authority, that I put myself under his scrutiny and authority? We don't even know each other.

Oh and by the way, it is interesting, in some cases, that the so-called covering ministries require a tithe or offerings to their ministry to continue being the covering. Otherwise if the pastor becomes unaffiliated, by not sending in his tithes, then he is somehow no longer "covered".

I feel this is an entrepreneurial scheme, thought up by men who can become rich by manipulating the Word of God. Are we in the ministry for God's glory and to build His kingdom, or are we in it to line our pockets?

The world already has plenty of reason to call the church hypocrites and complain about rich ministers, without these men making the problem worse. I could certainly see the need for fellowship among ministers and affiliations, but it seems money is always involved and the Kingdom of God can't go any farther because we won't do something for free.

People are even required to sign agreements, contracts, or covenants with the ministry leadership. As long as those tithes and offerings keep coming in I will be your covering.

The eldership in the body, are the spiritual advisors and counselors to that local body and the best scenario is to have accountability within the local body and with someone who knows you and respects you and loves you.

Covering is not a professional CEO of a mega-church a thousand miles away who only met you a couple of months ago or at a couple of seminars and shook your hand and engaged if five minutes of conversation.

Now, if that person is somebody you've known closely for some time and he is wise spiritually and a trusted friend, I see nothing wrong with confiding in that person or elder with whom you have a real relationship, especially if that person is the founding apostle to that local body. That is the type of ministry Paul had concerning the churches of Asia and Asia Minor.

One thing though, when Paul talked about taking up an offering, it was either for the poor persecuted Church in Jerusalem or for someone else. It was never for himself. Shame on these people who invent an ungodly system for power and monetary gain.

So much of the Church and the so-called leadership is corrupted by power and money, and oddly enough, I don't think many of them realize it. They have operated in the system for so long that they don't even see that it is wrong.

Never forget that your true covering is God and you are ultimately responsible to do the right thing with everyone you come in contact with.

If you choose to put yourself under a man or woman that you feel is older, wiser and would be trustworthy and a good confidante, that's up to you, but remember that they too are human and make mistakes like everyone else.

I'm well aware that ministers can have a connection with each other where one looks up to the other and advice is given. If fact, I have mentioned in this book that the elders in the church will and should be treated like fathers and mothers and spiritual mentors.

I've also written about the Rabbi duplicating himself with his disciples and that there is a certain respect given to the elder.

But, this business of "covering" is something else entirely, and I would re- examine your individual situation to see how it stands up Biblically.

I pray that you are not offended by the tone of this book. It is not written with that intention. I see this writing as an urgent call for scriptural New Testament Christianity to again rise up and come forth in the Church. If these are the last days before Jesus returns then the call to action should be sooner than later.

The institutional church seems to only be treading water spiritually at this present time rather than moving forward. I'm hoping someone will catch this vision and take whatever steps that is necessary to bring this new reformation into being.

Recommended Books

"The Reformation of the Glorious Church" by Juanita Newman

It can be found on Amazon.com or barnesandnoble.com.

"Pagan Christianity" by Frank Violas and George Barna

"Return to Authentic Christianity", chapter 11 is especially good.

"Reimaging Church" by Frank Viola

"The Holy Bible" written by the Holy Spirit

My contact information:
Glen Newman
Phone: 817-573-5763
Email: glenmnewman@aol.com
Website: www.pastorsmoveover.com
Address: P.O. Box 6772 Granbury, Texas 76049

Made in the USA
Lexington, KY
01 March 2013